El Salvador
Blood on All Our Hands

George Thurlow

STANSBURY
PUBLISHING
Chico, Ca.

El Salvador: Blood on All Our Hands
by George Thurlow

Copyright © 2024 by George Thurlow

ISBN 978-1-935807-75-9 pbk.
ISBN 978-1-935807-76-6 ePub

Library of Congress Control Number: 2024932915

First edition

Stansbury Publishing is an imprint of
Heidelberg Graphics

Front cover: George Thurlow being prepped for surgery at the Policlínica, San Salvador. Photo by John Newhagen.

Back cover: The scene near the Agua Caliente power plant just before journalists were shot. Photo by George Thurlow.

*Dedicated to the legacy of Gilberto Moran
and the courageous people of El Salvador.*

Contents

Part III

Preface: On a Bar Stool

I was in Tippy's bar, a San Francisco hole in the wall, in early 1981, when I met Carlos. He'd spent 12 years in El Salvador growing up.

I told him I was going in a few months, and he jabbed a finger at me and warned, "You better be careful." He lifted his shirt to his neck and pointed under his arm, toward a small purple line. Then he pointed to the other side of his rib cage: an identical scar.

"It went in here and out here," he explained with a certain pride in his voice about the path of the bullet. "I was sitting in a house on the corner in Ahuachapán, drinking coffee," he recalled, mimicking a dainty sip from a coffee cup, little finger extended. "Outside, a car squeals, and everyone looks up. It takes off. Then another car drives up and everybody is jumping on the floor, me too. The windows start crashing and there is a bump, bump, bump. When I get up, I feel something hot under my arm like I've never felt before. I see a dark hole in my sweater. Then I see the blood coming from beneath my shirt."

I asked him who did it.

"Drunk government soldiers," Carlos answered. He held an imaginary gun in his hand, waving it around the bar and making the sounds of rapid fire.

"Be careful," he warned again. "You must move among three groups in the country: the government—they are in the middle and don't know what to do; the people—they have nothing, work all day for two dollars with a boss watching to make sure they work; and finally, the people who own the country, The Families who do not want to give anything." He continued: "Revolution will come. It may take a long time."

I took the warning seriously and thought that even in a dark tavern in San Francisco, the fear and terror of the Salvadoran war was as visible as an in-and-out gunshot.

El Salvador was in the throes of a civil war between the Farabundo Marti National Liberation Front, or FMLN, which fought for an end to government repression and for land re-form, and an authoritarian government that had been installed in a bloodless military coup in 1979. The government, Car-los seemed to point out, was pulled between the demands of the poor and the powerful, conservative oligarchy, which was closely aligned with more hardline military leaders. But I should have heard something else in his words: a sense of people pushed to their limit, of others refusing to budge, and of violence everywhere. And though Carlos didn't name them, there was a fourth group involved: the U.S., funneling mon-ey and sophisticated arms to the government in the name of anti-communism, descending, as I was about to do, into a place it only partly understood.

Carlos's warning did not deter me. It prepared me to be a chronicler in what many believed would be a repeat of our di-sastrous adventure in Vietnam. But even the location of his scar would be a sign of what was to come.

Introduction: Another Vietnam

On November 27, 1980, weeks after Ronald Reagan won the election to be the incoming President of the United States, members of a prominent Salvadoran death squad kidnapped and murdered six leaders of the political opposition in El Salvador.

The kidnapping came during a press conference the leaders had organized at the offices of the archbishop of San Salvador. The killings seemed to signal an end to any hope for a peaceful solution to El Salvador's civil war.

Nearly one week later, on December 2, three American nuns—Ita Ford, Dorothy Kazel, and Maura Clarke—as well as an American religious worker, Jean Donovan, were kidnapped by Salvadoran soldiers as they rode from the airport to their destination outside the capital city of San Salvador. Then they were raped and killed. Their bodies were buried in a field outside the city.

It was clearly a message from the Salvadoran military, which was immediately implicated in the murders, that Americans who were perceived to be supporting Salvadoran reformers would be targeted. Catholic aid workers and their supporters in the U.S. were seen by the military and its conservative backers as aiding the poor, providing funds for social programs, and sympathetic to the aims of the guerrillas. And in a deeply Catholic nation, where nuns, even more than priests, are understood to symbolize the Catholic faith, it suggested that there would be no morals, no international standards, no accountability in the murders that would soon engulf this tiny Central American country.

In Woodland, California, a small farm town outside the state capital, I was an ambitious 29-year-old court and cop reporter chasing fire trucks and sitting through murder trials. I was ready for a big story.

Like many in my generation of reporters, I had read Michael Herr's *Dispatches*, marveled at Seymour Hersh's My Lai reports, and aspired to being a war correspondent. Vietnam had seared us all. Those who went came back forever changed. Those who stayed home were angry and defensive. It was The Story of our generation.

U.S. involvement in Vietnam was escalating when I was still a teenager, living at home in Visalia, CA. By my senior year in high school, 1968–1969, peace buttons were banned at our school and quickly became taboo treasures of secret rebellion. My more radical peers formed a Brown Beret chapter to push for Latino rights and were quickly suspended. When they returned, they preached loud and long about the evils of the Vietnam War and the disproportionate number of Latinos being drafted to fight while their white peers received "get out of Vietnam" cards in the form of student deferments. I admired their courage but was never an active participant. I was swept up in their passion, but not in marches or demonstrations. I was an observer.

When it came time to graduate, only a handful of us left Visalia to go to four-year colleges. College campuses, including UC Berkeley, were scenes of sometimes-violent protests against the war. Under pressure from my parents, I chose a peaceful, idyllic beach school: UC Santa Barbara. But UCSB was soon swept up in the same fervor as so many other campuses, and so was I. While there, I participated in my first sit-ins in my freshman year, protesting offshore oil drilling that had resulted in the worst U.S. environmental catastrophe to date off the coast of California. A Union Oil offshore well blew out and spilled four million gallons of crude oil onto Santa Barbara's pristine beaches.

I got my first taste of police pepper gas at a sit-in protesting a nighttime curfew in the UCSB college community of Isla Vista, which had become an anti-war hot spot with clashes between police and protesters. That same year, the Bank of America was torched in Isla Vista, burned to the ground with only the vault left standing. The pre-medical-school academic schedule I had set out for myself burned to cinders like the bank. I became a sociology major, like so many of my fellow protesters, tracking our progress toward what we hoped would be a political and social revolution.

At UCSB I also studied Proust, in a legendary year-long class reading the more than 2,200 pages of *Remembrance of Things Past*, which Professor Douwe Stuurman taught in his living room. Stuurman held interviews for the course in his office, probing to see how serious a student was, and why they wanted to read Proust. I told him I had decided to be a writer and heard this was the course to take, and he let me in. Reading Proust with him changed how I thought about memory, about what it means to live, about what words can do. Stuurman asserted week after week that only art could lead to everlasting life. It was not long before I realized that I was not going to achieve everlasting life with a short story, let alone a novel. But writing did allow me to be a silent observer of a wild world, then turn those observations into powerful words. It gave me freedom. It gave me a voice in a world filled with noise. It gave me a sense of my own power, and of potential influence. It gave me a byline.

When, after graduation, my friend Jeff von Kaenel recommended I start working as an unpaid volunteer proofreader for the *Santa Barbara News & Review*, I decided to go for it. Maybe, I imagined, I could eventually write stories, report on local issues, and help foster progressive ideas.

The paper was "owned" by its staff, with shares distributed based on longevity, not on position. We operated by a principle of "Rotation," wherein editors and writers would become ad salespeople, and ad guys would become writers. For those who chafed, there were always our "Criticism and Self-Criticism" sessions. Fortunately, all this rarely got in the way of putting out the newspaper, which was viewed in the community with a mixture of scorn and respect. And it forced me to take on tasks that I might not have—selling advertising in Isla Vista, delivering papers out of my VW van—to learn what it takes to get a writer's words in front of thousands of readers.

The *News & Review* was one of many alternative weekly papers across the country that drew energy from the Vietnam War protests, the broader cultural revolution, and a whole new stratum of advertising looking to profit from the spending of young boomers. Unlike many other alt weeklies, though, we made a fatal mistake: Rather than rely on that ad money, we charged our readers. In the beginning it was just a dime, but it killed us, that pile of silver dimes collected each Thursday.

Advertising money would have actually helped us succeed. Instead, we struggled, with nobody getting paid, the kids from wealthy backgrounds always able to buy cigarettes they shared with the rest of us, and the chips-and-salsa spread on production night considered a feast.

We had a crummy newsroom in a converted carpet cleaner's warehouse, and it was there I met Connie, one of a handful of paid typesetters. I had graduated from proofreader to paste-up guy to writer and ad salesman. I was covering the City Council beat, where I learned how to daydream while sitting upright. Connie was a tough, brilliant, petite, blonde feminist, and I fell in love. Somehow, our dreams of the future merged. She wanted to go to law school and was accepted as one of the few women at UC Davis School of Law. Through a friend of a friend, I heard of an opening for a crime reporter at the Woodland *Daily Democrat*, just 10 miles away from Davis. I applied and got the job.

We packed our stuff, and what I believed was my dream life was about to begin—until we pulled into Woodland in the middle of summer and realized how hellish our tiny, roasting shack of a rental was. Things got better when we moved to a little 1930s bungalow on a shaded street, with a view from the porch chairs of huge rice storage silos on the horizon.

We settled into a rhythm, punctuated by occasional gin and tonics on the front porch with our neighbors, Bill and Doris, or visits from Richard, the newspaper ad salesman who lived behind us and would pop over now and again for a puff. Mostly, though, our days were shaped by work. I would head out by 5:30 a.m. to make sure I beat my boss into the office. Connie set off for law school later in the morning and wasn't home until dinner. I would be in bed by 10, but she stayed up until 1 a.m. typing up her lecture notes.

We were together but always apart. We put off talk of the future and loved our beautiful German Shepherd. For both of us, we were setting the foundation for our ultimate careers and adventures. Typing law all night, writing courtroom stories all day.

The tiny newsroom at the Woodland *Daily Democrat* was shaped like a bowling alley with desks lining the gutters, and when I first walked in, I was in way over my head. In Santa Barbara, I'd had a week to noodle stories. Now I had to write multiple obituaries, arrest reports, false fire alarms, burglaries, DUIs, and everything that needed a rewrite every day. But I was, at least, more reliable than the guy I had succeeded: He had a drinking problem, and the bottle was not a good mixer with the early shift.

My boss at the paper was a devout Catholic and third-generation publisher, Kenneth Leake. By the time he came in at 6 a.m. every morning, I was already banging away on photo captions from the wirephotos that came spewing off the machine, each one marked by a bell. (One bell meant wake up, somebody was doing something. Multiple bells meant a president had been assassinated.) My first deadline was at 8 a.m., and the paper—on the press by 10 a.m.—was delivered to driveways before noon. We were one of the last hybrid morning-afternoon papers, and it meant I had to learn to be quick—and then quicker. To not be fancy or frilly. Just sleek and factual.

Once the morning's stories were filed, I would head out into the cold, foggy, and often dark Yolo County mornings to the police station for crime reports, to the fire station for news of emergencies, and finally to the county jail for bookings. All were within two blocks of each other. Then I'd call the mortuaries for obituaries. But my main beat was the county courthouse. It was here I learned to report, and to witness human nature at its lows and occasional highs.

There were slick defense attorneys, heroic judges, and a bailiff who later turned out to be a perv. There was Luis Rodriguez, the enigmatic cop killer; people who'd murdered cab drivers for spare change; nice kids who shot somebody without thinking; and seemingly bad kids who really were good inside. They were murderers, drug dealers, and stupid drunks. All there, all exposed. And just when I thought I had seen it all, there was Sluggo, the Hells Angel, accused of slitting a rival biker's throat.

Sluggo was alleged to have killed a rival after they got into an argument at a biker bar. Like many killings at that time, the murder occurred in Sacramento County, but perpetrators like Sluggo, a.k.a. Douglas Fellows, would take the body over the county line, into Yolo County, where it was assumed that the police were less vigilant and killers could more easily escape detection.

During Sluggo's trial in Yolo County, I was allowed into evidentiary hearings in the judge's chambers. In one hearing, the prosecutor wanted to introduce a large display case from Sluggo's house on which he had affixed knives of all sizes and uses—evidence, the prosecutor said, that the jury needed to see to understand why Sluggo had slit the victim's throat, ear to ear. The judge decided the collection was too prejudicial to show the jury, but I ran the story anyway—after all, it had all been on the record. The defense attorney went ballistic. His remedy: Call me as a witness in the case and thus bar me from sitting in court and reporting.

Defense attorney David Weiner was blistering in his interview with *The Sacramento Bee*. "I was not remanding him because he was a reporter, but because of who he is. I don't approve of the way the man abuses the facts," Weiner was quoted as saying. "The statements in the paper were abusive and grossly distorted of the facts heard here, and are detrimental to my client's case." But my inspirational publisher came to my defense: "We have a lot of confidence as far as George Thurlow is concerned—in his accuracy and in his ability to tell a straight story without prejudice."

The judge agreed. The *Los Angeles Times* ran a photo of me sitting in the courthouse hallway with a front-page story, and the judge changed his mind. Sluggo was convicted of involuntary manslaughter, and I sometimes wonder if he still holds a grudge. Some observers thought I was naïve and reckless in taking on a Hells Angel and their powerful defense attorney. It would not be the last time I would be so described.

Back at the office, Leake was stern, stiff, and a newsman through and through. I'll always remember the day he threw onto my desk, in his typical gruff manner, a clipping he had torn from a neighboring county newspaper. It was a brief account of a run-of-the-mill drug arrest. But what caught my eye was the scofflaw: It was Leake's own grown son. "Get it in today's paper," was all he said.

When I had finished the piece, the copy editor was frantic that I was going to publish this damaging story about the owner's son. "What's this?" he wailed. "Ken wants it in today's paper," I said. There was no room for nepotism, or shame, to cloud one's sense of obligation to your readers.

I learned other lessons there too. When our copy editor hustled me out the door to take pictures of a fatal car crash on a nearby country road, just months after I'd come on board, I grabbed my trusty Konica—bought from a pawn shop in Santa Barbara—and headed out to the scene. When I arrived, adrenaline pumping, I witnessed what was left of a Porsche convertible mashed against a tree along the road, with a dead boy sprawled next to it. As I started snapping, the CHP officer looked at me with disdain, but I figured a dead body and a mashed sports car were the ingredients of enterprise journalism.

When I got back, my camera was taken and rushed into the darkroom. A little bit later, the editor wandered over to my desk with the proof sheet. His voice was firm: "We don't run photos of bodies." Instead, we run photos of horrific car wrecks with blankets over the bodies. We conjure all the mayhem, but tradition says we don't desecrate the dead. This is a particularly American tradition. In Third World countries, the bodies are full-face on the cover of the local newspapers.

Not that everything was about consideration for the victims. Late in the morning of September 25, 1978, the AP bells started clanging: PSA Flight 182 from Sacramento to San Diego had crashed, killing everybody aboard and people on the ground. It was the worst air disaster in the history of California aviation and, at the time, the worst air disaster in American history.

The PSA flight was descending into Lindbergh Field, one of the most harrowing domestic airports to land at, when a Cessna with two experienced pilots practicing visual landings hit the PSA plane.

When the passenger manifest came over the wire some hours later, there was one victim from Davis, the community down the road where we actually produced a separate edition. My editor and the publisher came to my desk with one firm instruction: Track down the victim (later identified as Carl Miller) and call his family. And say what? I wondered. "Ask them how they feel" was the stock response.

It was my first taste of the worst of American journalism. Stick a microphone or a camera in the face of a grieving family member and ask them how they feel. I said I did not want the assignment. I was told there was no choice. I stalled, obfuscated, and punted. Finally, the desk editor did the call.

Never forget that American journalism can be petty, arrogant, and unfeeling. And what did we get out of that interview? Nothing. Grief and tears.

I saw a related impulse at the courtroom when I was covering the trial of Darrell Rich for the serial killing of four women and the rape of five others. He had variously beat, strangled, and shot his victims, and after raping his 11-year-old neighbor Annette Selix, he threw her off a 105-foot highway bridge over Shasta Lake. During court recesses, some of my colleagues seemed eager to go up to the evidence table and study the murder scene photos. The one of Selix, they said, was particularly disturbing. She had not died on impact; instead, she curled into a fetal position, lived for some time, and then died.

I never could bring myself to join them, even though the lure was powerful. It was another sad view of my profession. Journalists are the chroniclers of our lives and our society. But they are voyeurs, fascinated by the macabre and the revolting.

I was no different but did not want to be associated with this type of journalism, so I held back. A quiet observer.

Darrell Rich was convicted, and in 2000, after 20 years on death row, he became one of the last inmates in California to be executed. His case changed me in profound ways. The clarity I'd felt as a campus protester was gone. You could sit in a courtroom just a few feet from a monster who killed and raped and looked like the neighbor down the street. I'd been against capital punishment before, but now I felt confused by it all. More importantly, the world seemed darker. Horrific actions didn't just take place far away. They were real, and close to home. I never figured out why Darrell Rich was such a monster. Some said it was his mother. Others said it was because of no father in the family. Still others just said he was a bad seed. We journalists had no answers. We just stared at the murder scene photos.

In 1980, Connie graduated law school and left Woodland for a great job in the San Francisco City Attorney's office. I stayed behind at the *Daily Democrat* during what I eventually realized was a kind of slow-motion breakup. I wanted more—from life, from my career—and I thought international reporting might help me get it.

My years in Woodland had coincided with a rightward drift in American politics. Ronald Reagan was ascending from governor of California to president. While he brandished a brilliant smile and the affability of a favorite grandfather, his politics were hard-edged and unsympathetic. He went after those on welfare, called for joining authoritarian leaders to fight communism, and saw crime as America's most pressing problem.

His campaign for president included the warning that the revolution in Nicaragua and the brewing civil war in El Salvador required the U.S. to take military action. This seemed a repeat of the slow descent into the Vietnam War quagmire. When President Reagan came into office, he openly retreated from the Carter policies in Central America and called for massive infusions of war materials for the Salvadoran military. (Later he would secretly arm and support the war of the Contras against the Nicaraguan Sandinista government.)

President Carter had tried to navigate the tricky relationship with an authoritarian Salvadoran government, its powerful military, and the growing danger of secret death squads. Reagan offered wholehearted support for a military solution to a 50-year struggle by the Salvadoran poor to improve their living standards. He fired U.S. Ambassador to El Salvador Robert E. White for being soft on communism and began rattling his saber in Central America. When Reagan's new Ambassador to the United Nations, Jeane Kirkpatrick, was informed of the November 1980 murder and mutilation of the six Salvador opposition leaders, she told *The New York Times*, "People who choose to live by the sword can expect to die by it." Kirkpatrick believed that supporting authoritarian governments who committed human rights violations was critical in the fight against communism.

After the December 2, 1980, kidnapping, rape, and murder of the three American nuns and a churchwoman, President Carter, still in office, cut U.S. aid to El Salvador. But Reagan, awaiting inauguration, had already signaled his coming administration's intentions. They would be comfortable with the blood flowing more and more swiftly in Central America. The hard-right thinkers fueling his administration's policy—Jeane Kirkpatrick, Secretary of State Alexander Haig, and Oliver North—would not be swayed by domestic dissent nor intimidated by a strong popular uprising. They intended to make El Salvador a battlefield in a proxy war against the Soviet Union.

Very early on, some of these extraordinarily powerful politicians—Reagan, Kirkpatrick, and Haig—knew the Salvadoran government was covering up for the killers of the nuns, opposition leaders, and union members. They even assisted with the cover-up. Kirkpatrick even went so far as to say that the nuns were guerrilla sympathizers, implying their deaths were deserved, while Haig claimed the nuns had tried to run a roadblock.

New York Times reporter Raymond Bonner, the dean of American reporters in El Salvador, wrote a jarring piece for *The Atlantic* magazine in 2016 that profiled the low-level American embassy official, 26-year-old Carl Gettinger, who in 1981 had found a source in the Salvadoran National Guard who gave him the names of those involved in the murder of the nuns. The information was shared with Salvadoran government officials and the head of the National Guard, but no action was taken. The implicated National Guard soldiers were not indicted until 1984. They were convicted and sentenced to 30 years in prison, but released in the late 1990s.

In 1981, the full scope of U.S. collusion was not yet known, but it was clear that a military buildup was underway and the first discussion of U.S. military advisors was occurring. I felt it was time for me to go. I wanted to be there first. I wanted to report what was becoming another Vietnam.

In California newspapers, there was only some interest in the tiny, impoverished country of El Salvador. By early April 1981, I had met with reporters who had been there, read everything I could find about the region, and interviewed exiles and experts. I walked into Ken Leake's office and asked him if he would consider the two weeks of vacation I had earned as a "working vacation" so that I could publish my reporting in the *Daily Democrat*.

He smiled, then said, "Sure." Anything written by a local reporter was better than the wire any day of the week. Besides, he told me, the killing of the nuns had bothered him. A few days later, he quietly put an envelope in my hand that held a check for $1,000, a princely expense account in those days. That night, I started packing. In a bold move, I went to the police chief in Woodland and asked if I could borrow his personal bulletproof vest. He obliged, though I knew that if I brought it back with a dent in it, there would be hell to pay.

Part I

April 26, 1981

When I landed in El Salvador on April 26, 1981, I was sweating profusely in the bulletproof vest my local police chief had loaned me. The customs officials, in bright-red berets, were intent on going through everything I had. They looked over my camera and inspected every article of clothing I'd packed. If they'd known about the vest, they probably would have confiscated it as possible guerrilla gear, but they didn't seem to notice. They did, however, rifle through the items I was to bring to a Salvadoran nun, Rosa Lillia, courtesy of a nun I'd met at City Hall in San Francisco while doing background for the trip. She'd given me a bottle of shampoo for Rosa, a Charlie Brown book for a seminarian who was learning English, and an envelope containing a $1,000 check to support the Catholics' work with refugees and orphans. She had also given me a check for $100 she wanted me to deliver as cash as a personal gift. Her words had chilled me: "You are never secure—not in your hotel, not in the street, never. Always be careful who you talk to. Do not trust anybody."

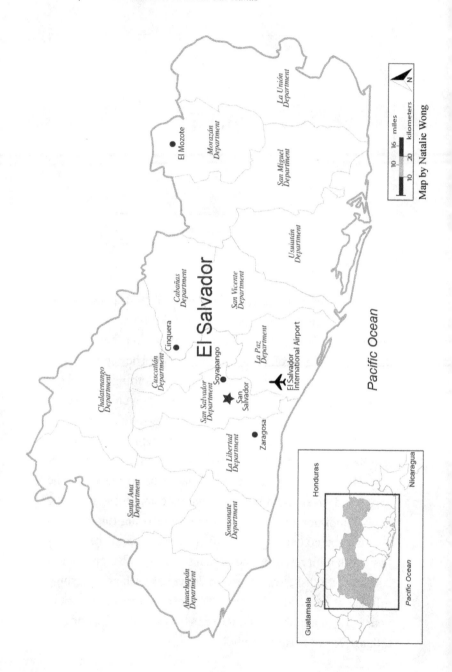

Map by Natalie Wong

Happily, customs let me and my belongings through. Outside, I was terrified. A correspondent I'd talked with in the U.S. had told me, of driving through San Salvador, "Keep your windows rolled down so that if the soldiers yell or whistle, you hear them and stop immediately. Otherwise, they will shoot you."

Dozens of cab drivers were beseeching me to go with them, but would one of them kidnap me? If so, nobody would even know. I opted for a communal bus, thinking that if anything happened, there would at least be witnesses. On board, the driver immediately began pestering me to sell her my dollars. She told me I would need the local currency. I declined her offer and settled in. A kindly older man across the aisle told me the government only lets citizens buy $500 in dollars per year. It was an effort to keep valuable dollars in the country, rather than allowing them to be invested elsewhere.

He told me that he had just dropped off his son for a plane trip to New York. "He is 21 and finished school," he explained. "There are no factories open, no jobs, and all the troubles," he said with a shrug. He said the "man on the street" supports the new American president, Ronald Reagan. "But not the guerrillas."

The last to board the bus was Ana, from Santa Ana. She was coming from Los Angeles, where she had left her husband, an American. She had become an American citizen, and like so many Salvadorans, she was ambivalent about her native country. On the one hand, she pointed out, it is filled with lush, tropical forests; majestic volcanoes; and many kind people. But as we passed peasants walking on the highway with heads bowed, she murmured, "They are all so sad." She turned to me and asked, "Are you scared?"

"A little," I responded, trying to be brave.

"So am I," she said.

The drive from the airport took about 45 minutes, and when we made it into San Salvador, I headed for the Camino Real Hotel. Before the war intensified, the Camino Real was one of the capital's most luxurious and expensive hotels. Business meetings, quinceañeras, and official government events were held in its courtyard.

But now, it was ghostly. Reporters and their entourages were the only occupants of what had been the biggest and best hotel in El Salvador. The week before I arrived, a bomb had gone off across the street at the front door of the Banco de América (no relation to our Bank of America), and it had blown out a number of the windows of the rooms on the street side of the hotel. At check-in, I was assigned to a room on the garden side, away from the street.

When I had started to plan my journey, the Associated Press's bureau chief, Joseph Frazier, was my contact. The *Daily Democrat* was an AP paper and, as a client, we were granted the courtesy of his services upon my arrival in San Salvador.

But just as I was arriving, Frazier was taking a much-needed break from what was considered one of the most dangerous news assignments of the early '80s. All my efforts in advance to set up a mentor in San Salvador fell apart at the last minute. I was going to be on my own.

(Frazier's account of his time in El Salvador can be found in his perceptive book *El Salvador Could Be Like That*.)

In addition to the AP, there was one other major global wire service: United Press International. UPI was the stepchild and sick cousin of the international news industry. But while the Associated Press had far more members (news organizations bought membership to get the daily feed), the UPI had the energy of vast legions of freelancers who wanted to make it in the competitive world of foreign news.

My paper did subscribe to UPI photos, and I figured our subscription allowed me to call on the UPI's man in El Salvador, John Newhagen, for help and advice. I figured wrong.

I first met Newhagen in a hallway in the Camino Real, as he was running down the hall toward his room, Room 204. It was a room that journalists at some point in their stay at the Camino Real seemed to visit for information, news, or comfort. Newhagen was not the sage leader of the Salvadoran press corps; he was the frenetic information collector and connector. As he passed me, I tried to introduce myself. It was pathetic. Newhagen had seen legions of young reporters like me arrive in El Salvador and just as quickly depart. He had files to send. I would be gone soon.

That night, the bar was hopping with journalists and a handful of businesspeople. Outside, there was an eerie quiet as the military-imposed curfew approached.

I was one of many freelancers. Another, Alex, was busy trying to determine from the other reporters whether one part of the countryside had been napalmed. Nobody seemed to know.

A freelance photographer working for the international photo service Magma was complaining that nobody was buying pictures these days. El Salvador is out of the news, he complained. "All they want is action death shots," asserted another freelancer. Unlike in the U.S., there was no moral prohibition about showing the Salvadoran dead, whether they be blown up or shot in the back of the head.

I met Steve Patten, a CBS correspondent, smoking cheap, poorly rolled local cigars in the Camino Real bar. I also met his crew: cameraman Tony Foresta and soundman Larry Bullard. I asked if I could tag along with the CBS crew the next day, but I was told CBS had a strict policy against taking anybody along. They did, however, invite me to dinner. We went for pizza at a popular spot just across the street behind the Camino Real.

This also happened to be the first meeting in months of the Salvadoran Press Association—a loose-knit organization of journalists who needed official-looking press passes. The main topic at the restaurant: lousy service in the hotel. Only one elevator works, complained one journalist. And room service takes forever. Finally, people were concerned about a colonel who had come into the hotel wearing his gun and acting "out of control." Somebody said he'd fondled a male reporter.

My brilliant question: "What does the military do?"

There was laughter all around. "They hide a lot," replied one veteran network cameraman.

Another quipped, "It's a known guerrilla tactic to delay room service."

As dark began to fall, even the most resolute journalists began to make plans to hustle back to the hotel. The dawn-to-dusk curfew, meant to deny guerrillas the cover of night, instead was a convenient cover for death squads roaming the streets in pickups and SUVs, never being stopped by military patrols. Being caught out after dark, for journalists and average Salvadorans, was considered a death sentence.

After dinner, we retreated to the NBC suite on the third floor of the hotel. It was packed with editing and sound equipment but became a makeshift movie-screening room at night. The program this evening? A Betamax version of *Apocalypse Now*, which had only been released two years earlier, in 1979.

About a dozen journalists were there, drinking and smoking pot, trying to relax after another day of avoiding death and getting a story that might never even make it on the air or into print. Watching one of the most captivating movies about the Vietnam War on the third floor of the Camino Real, where occasional gunshots could be heard in the distance, was, to say the least, eerie. The movie is filled with crazy people, brutal killings, and a powerful message about the insanity of war. It allowed the journalists in the room to turn into audience members, no longer responsible for covering the war, but it also reminded them all that come morning, death would fill the streets.

Dial Torgerson, one of the most respected foreign journalists of the decade, was lying on the bed sipping a gin and tonic. He alone was not smoking. Torgerson was considered one of the premier "firemen" in the American foreign press corps. His career at the *Los Angeles Times* included coverage of topics as diverse as the Charles Manson murders and the rise of American financial buccaneer Kirk Kerkorian. He had reported from Africa and later the Middle East and gained a reputation as a reporter who was fearless and thoughtful. Just a month before I found myself in a room with him, he had been made Mexico City bureau chief for the *Times*, in charge of all Latin American coverage. We never spoke, and our paths never crossed in El Salvador again, but I was amazed to find myself in the same room with him and other heavy hitters in American foreign journalism.

I had been reading Torgerson's work to prepare for my own trip. I was most interested in a piece in the *Times*, just two weeks before I'd arrived, profiling a Cleveland priest, Kenneth Myers, who ran an orphanage in Zaragoza, just outside San Salvador. The piece was so good I was determined I would visit the orphanage and also interview Myers. Here was an American who had dedicated his life to helping the most needy: Salvador's abandoned and lost children.

April 27, 1981

I planned to set out for the orphanage on my first full day in the country, but I had other stops to make too. Gen. Jose Guillermo Garcia, the defense minister and commander of all security forces, and Gen. Carlos Eugenio Vides Casanova, head of the National Guard and later the defense minister, were presiding over a press conference at the military headquarters, Estado Mejor, in San Salvador.

Estado Mejor was a sprawling military compound with armed

Gen. Jose Guillermo Garcia was implicated in ordering or covering up some of El Salvador's worst killings. To his right, Col. Carlos Eugenio Vides Casanova, who oversaw the coverup of the killing of the four American churchwomen. Photo by George Thurlow.

guards at every entrance. The press conference was in a nondescript conference room that had quickly filled with journalists, eager to get Garcia's response to reports that the military might have been involved in the killing of the four American churchwomen.

Garcia was a rotund man with a large black mole on his chin that looked like the devil had planted it there. I saw the same evil I had seen in Darrell Rich's face. Garcia was adamant that he and Casanova knew nothing about the killing of the four American churchwomen just a few months earlier. He told the large gathering of reporters that he and the other military leaders were "waiting" for a report from the FBI with their conclusions on the murders. At the time, the FBI suspected that the Salvadoran National Guard troops were involved. Garcia added, "We are expecting to announce soon the results in this matter." He concluded, "We want to do it the legal way and correctly." A few weeks later, it was announced that six National Guard troops had been detained for the killings. They were all subsequently released.

Garcia went on to say that the situation in the countryside was "tranquil" and that El Salvador's fight against communism was going well. He framed it as part of a "worldwide" struggle against communism, and said the only fighting was in the department of Morazán. But reports in the local media had indicated there was fighting and bombing going on throughout the countryside. Even the pro-government newspaper *El Diario* reported that guerrilla attacks were on the upswing. In the week I was in El Salvador, two bridges were bombed, army garrisons around the country were attacked, and guerrillas attacked the power station in Soyapango.

Later, I visited the U.S. Embassy. Flyers with a photo of a bearded man, John J. Sullivan—along with pleas for information about his whereabouts—were everywhere. Sullivan, a freelance writer from *Penthouse* magazine, had disappeared on December 28, 1980. According to an article that ran the following month in the local media, "a day after he had registered in a capital hotel … he was leaving to find a cup of coffee" and was not seen again.

As far as anyone could tell at the time, Sullivan's mistake had been to book a room not at the Camino Real, but at the Sheraton. "No journalist checked into the Sheraton," Viviana Moreno, a veteran photographer and later a TV "fixer," recalled years later. (Fixers were the locals who set up interviews, arranged travel logistics, and got journalists out of trouble.) Even I had quickly taken the Sheraton off my list when I checked out the hotel situation. First of all, it was where the U.S. was stationing its 56 military "trainers" in what Torgerson had reported was a heavily fortified wing. Second, there were widespread rumors that there were also numerous "spooks," sent by the Reagan administration in excess of the cap Congress had approved, staying there. Al Venter profiles some of them in his book *El Salvador: Dance of the Death Squads*: American mercenaries, carrying U.S. Embassy identification, who flew Salvadoran bombers or led elite Salvador anti-insurgency military units. "We would see the same people later in the Middle East, later in Honduras," Moreno recalled. Third, the Sheraton was owned by Hans Crist, a businessman holding both Salvadoran and West German citizenship. Crist was known to have ties to the death squads operating across El Salvador. And at the time, death squads and the Salvadoran military felt they had free rein to not only brutally kill their own people, but to go after Americans—including, people guessed, John Sullivan.

The death squads operated at night, during the military-imposed curfew. They were supported by wealthy right-wing business leaders and given free passage by the military and police. Their targets were almost always young men and women, often union, student, or community leaders. The victims were dragged from their homes by masked men, loaded into

Jeep Cherokees or pickup trucks, and taken away. Their mutilated bodies were often found the next day. A favorite tactic was to cut men's penises off and stick them in the victim's mouth, as well as carving the initials of the death squads on the breasts of women. Grotesque sexual violence seemed to be one of the death squads' trademarks.

Years later, declassified State Department documents indicated that U.S. officials, including those in the Reagan Administration, knew the death squads were being funded by conservative Salvadoran elites and operated with the blessing of the military. But U.S. officials were afraid to hold the Salvadoran government accountable, believing it would hurt the war on the guerrillas.

Just three months before my arrival in San Salvador, two U.S. labor union advisors had been shot and killed by unknown assailants as they sat in the Sheraton's coffee shop. Witnesses said Crist gave the orders to shoot. He was arrested as the instigator but never prosecuted. Killed in the shooting were Michael Hammer, 42, of Potomac, Maryland, and Mark Pearlman, 36, of Seattle, Washington. Hammer and Pearlman were with the AFL-CIO's American Institute for Free Labor Development and were advising Salvadoran government and civilian nonprofit leaders on land reform techniques.

Land reform was a lightning-rod issue in El Salvador, where thousands of acres of land had been taken from rich landowners for redistribution to peasants. Moderates in El Salvador supported the land reform as the only way to placate poor Salvadorans and diminish revolutionary fervor. The right, however, framed it as part of an international communist conspiracy supported by leftist Americans, including members of the Catholic Church.

The current social order in El Salvador emerged in the nineteenth century, when large coffee plantations began to take over subsistence farms. Peasants who had grown corn, maize, and vegetables on their small plots were forced off their land and, to survive, took jobs as seasonal coffee pickers paid by the hour. This in turn created a new landless class of very poor workers who followed the coffee harvest around the country, but only worked during the short harvest season. Their labor helped a new elite, symbolized by the infamous 14 Families who would control the country's economy for more than 70 years, come to power—but not without considerable discontent.

By the 1930s, there were strikes, mass marches, and violence across the countryside. The elite answered them by ramping up the repression, including the 1932 *Matanza*, or "massacre," ordered by Gen. Maximiliano Hernandez Martinez, the military strongman who had taken power in a 1931 coup. Throughout the decade, more than 30,000 people were killed by members of the military and their paramilitary organization, ORDEN. Members of the indigenous Pipil tribe were targeted. Peasant leaders were hanged in town squares. Agustin Farabundo Marti, who emerged as the titular leader of various peasant organizations, became a leftist hero, and half a century later, his name would be adopted by diverse groups who took up arms against the military oligarchy as the Farabundo Marti National Liberation Front, or FMLN.

A 1979 coup installed more moderate members of the military

in power, in a junta that cut across political lines. The new government called for, among other things, the nationalization of foreign trade in coffee and sugar; an investigation of political acts of violence; and land reform. But these measures were carried out with limited success. Land reform occurred in some areas near San Salvador, but not in the countryside where the conservative oligarchies were most entrenched. The hardliners in the military and their conservative political allies in the oligarchy continued the repression against labor unions, peasant organizations, and intellectuals, and the new junta seemed powerless to stop the killing. Until 1982, military juntas ruled during the most intense repression of the war.

El Salvador's Archbishop Oscar Romero in a famous sermon on March 23, 1980, called on members of the military to disobey orders to kill their fellow countrymen and called for an end of the repression of popular organizations. The next day, Romero was assassinated in his private chapel by members of a right-wing death squad with ties to far-right military officers.

A week later, the U.S. approved $5.7 million in new military aid to prop up the military government. The military aid swelled to $90 million under the Carter Administration in 1980. In early 1981, newly elected President Reagan escalated the war: He sent 55 official U.S. military advisors to train the Salvadoran Army. By 1987, that number had ballooned to more than 150 advisors, as well as an unknown number of "spooks."

In El Salvador, no one, it seemed, was safe.

John J. Sullivan's remains were found a year and a half after his disappearance, thanks to a series of letters his family had received from an anonymous Salvadoran who claimed to have been part of a death squad that kidnapped Sullivan. The letters gave detailed information about Sullivan's appearance, the amount of money he was carrying, and the ways he had been kept in a cell, interrogated, tortured, and killed. Evidently, security forces had been complicit in his disappearance. In July 1982, a grave was dug at the site of a map that had been provided to the family, and it contained what the forensic pathologist Dr. Frederick Zugibe, in his book *Dissecting Death*, described as a "small pile of crushed and splintered bone fragments." Tense back-and-forth discussions between the Salvadoran government, the U.S. government, and the Sullivan family followed; the Salvadorans did not want to release the remains, but eventually did so. When Zugibe examined them in 1983, he concluded that Sullivan was either killed, or dismembered after being killed, by having an explosive charge wrapped around him and then set off. The force of the explosion blew apart Sullivan's head and face and much of his upper body.

None of this was clear when I arrived in the country in April 1981, but the risk of disappearance was. Being an American would not protect you from the death squads. You needed to look out for yourself.

I wasn't great at this. On my first morning in San Salvador, I had walked out the Camino Real front door, motioned to a cab driver who was lolling near the hotel entrance, and given him directions to the church where I hoped to find the nun I'd been sent to see with my $1,000 check. The taxi sped across town and pulled up to a small church with large, ornate wooden doors, both firmly closed. He waited as I knocked. Finally, a young boy opened one of the doors. When I asked for the nun, he said, "She's not here." When I asked when she would return, he responded, "I don't know." When I persisted, his answers grew even more terse, and his eyes told me that a gringo at his door was not a good thing. I got in the cab and headed back to the Camino Real.

That night, I shared my story at the Camino Real bar with several veteran journalists. They were flabbergasted. "Don't ever take a cab from in front of the hotel!" they yelled. "Those are all government agents!" A Salvadoran added, "Where do you think they learned their English?!"

I realized, with horror, that I'd exposed the nun and her church to possible government harassment, or worse.

"If you need a cab, kid," said one old-timer, "run across the street and flag one down that looks like they are hurrying somewhere else. And another thing—don't trust anybody here. Not in the hotel. Not outside. Half the people who work in this hotel are guerrilla agents; the other half are government security. They are all spying on us."

The chief correspondent of the NBC TV crew recommended I hire Salvadoran Gilberto Moran. He said they had used Gilberto as both a driver and an interpreter. It was clear that I needed both. My rudimentary Spanish was fine in restaurants, worthless in Salvadoran Army checkpoints. I planned, the next morning, to rent a car and pay Gilberto to drive it.

April 28, 1981

After I set things up with Gilberto, we went together to the enclosed compound of the Catholic orphanage in Zaragoza, about 20 miles outside San Salvador, that I had read about in Torgerson's piece. I had made an appointment to talk with Father Kenneth Myers, hoping he would give me an American perspective on the war—and thinking that the story of caring for Salvadoran war orphans was worth spreading—but he was running late.

Gilberto and I sprawled under the shade of a tree in the yard, pawing through snacks we had packed that morning. We shot the breeze for a little, and then he declared: "I want to use the rental car tonight. I want you to loan it to me. I'll bring it back tomorrow."

This was a bit of a shocker. Renting a car in a war zone was about the edge of my bravery. As I signed the paperwork that morning, I had thoughts of returning it at the end of the day with bullet holes, smashed-in fenders, and assorted broken parts from potted roads and yawning ditches. And those were just daytime fears: There was a shoot-on-sight military curfew at night. Why, I asked, did he need the car that night?

He wouldn't answer directly. He told me about his sister, a political activist who was in prison. He told me about his wife and his daughter. His wife worked at a local maquiladora, manufacturing parts for a huge U.S. electronics firm.

I was suspicious. He seemed to be hinting that a guerrilla operation needed to go on that night. I guessed that he was government and trying to set me up, so that I could serve as an example of the supposedly impartial journalists who were secretly or not-so-secretly sympathetic to guerrillas.

I told him I would decide later and changed the subject to voting. Under the pretext that everybody in El Salvador had to have some identification to vote, I asked to see his—hoping that, as he got it out, I could check for any sort of government badge peeking out of his wallet.

His Salvadoran identification card was standard issue, but something caught my attention: He was born on November 10, 1951, the same day I was born. It was eerie. Here we were, sitting under a tree in an orphanage in the world's most dangerous place, and we were connected in some cosmic way. Was this a sign, or just a statistical coincidence? I hoped it was a special karma connecting us like brothers.

When Father Ken arrived, he took us on a quick tour of the orphanage. There were more than 100 children of all ages,

Gilberto Moran hanging out with orphans at the Zaragoza orphanage. Photo by George Thurlow.

some in classrooms, some running around on the playground. A group of pre-kindergarteners were eating lunch. Most of the children came from rural areas where their parents had been arrested or disappeared.

Gilberto mugged for my camera with the kids. He was clearly enjoying himself, both as official translator for an American reporter, and as a chronicler of his people's plight. I liked him a lot. He was funny, smart, and kind to the people we met. And he knew what his job was: Drive me somewhere safely and, once there, tell me what people were saying and why they were saying it. Most important, steer us clear of military and security forces.

Hoping to make up for my blunder at the church the day before,

Faces of war. Some of the 190 children housed at an orphanage run by Father Kenneth Myers from the Cleveland Diocese. Photo by George Thurlow.

I asked Father Ken if he had ever heard of Rosa Lillia, the nun to whom I was to deliver materials from San Francisco. "Oh yes, she is here today," he responded. When I met her, I finally delivered the book, shampoo, check, and cash. I later learned that she was a leader of the Sisters of Divine Providence in San Salvador, and she led several church groups investigating the killing of civilians by the death squads.

As we headed back into the city that afternoon, I told Gilberto I couldn't let him use the car. I felt guilty turning him down, but too anxious to do anything else. The good news, I told him, was that I would be able to use him a lot during the next 10 days.

I wondered what the impact of seeing all the religious workers that day, tending to the orphans, had on Gilberto. I asked him if he believed in God. "No," he said, "I believe in the trees, in the flowers, in the land, in the sky. I believe in myself."

He shared that his wife wanted to get out of El Salvador, to flee to the United States. But he resisted, wanted to stay, wanted to "fight." He said it again: "I believe in myself."

When we parted, I told him to meet me at the hotel the next morning. I returned the rental car at the hotel.

That night, I went back to the bar at the Camino Real. I was beginning to learn what other American and European journalists in foreign postings already knew: In the bar, you find out what is important, what is real, and whom to trust.

Harry Mattison, who was freelancing for *Time* magazine, clued me into some of it. A year after I met him, he received

A refugee family driven from their village by the war and living with thousands of others in a Catholic Church–sponsored refugee camp in San Salvador. Photo by George Thurlow.

the Robert Capa Gold Medal for Photography with the description of his work as "The Best Foreign Reporting Requiring Exceptional Courage and Enterprise," but in the bar that night, he described himself as a former poet who drove a cab in New York while also "humping sheetrock" to make enough money to travel the world as a photographer.

He'd been in El Salvador off and on for 14 months, with time in Nicaragua before that. He pointed to an Argentinian girlfriend as the inspiration for his choice to work in Latin America. He complained, but with a sense of humor, about his $30 a month retainer and the $175 per photo *Time* paid him. His expenses: $3,000 a month—thus, the cab driving and sheetrock humping. He had grown to love El Salvador, though, and as he put it to me and the other newbies in the crowd, "If you don't love my sister, fuck off, brother."

Still, he admitted, honesty in this country could be dangerous. To "last" in El Salvador, he went on, "It's better to have the umbrella of the right and flirt with the left."

Some drunk Salvadorans interrupted us. "All you guys do is shit," one said, pointing to us journalists. "What about trying land reform in Texas?" We ignored them, but the tension was left in the room. We were the outsiders telling Salvadorans about land reform and poverty and human rights. Those who drank in the swank Camino Real bar were not sympathetic to our journalism.

Our conversation turned to the disappearance of Catholic priest Roy Bourgeois, who had come to El Salvador with a CBS Chicago affiliate news crew, and had vanished two days before—the same day I'd checked into the Camino Real. He'd talked his way onto the trip by offering himself as an interpreter. He was fluent in Spanish and a Vietnam veteran with a Purple Heart. But when he walked across the street from the hotel toward a drugstore, he didn't come back, and no one knew what had happened to him.

Many journalists thought that he, like Sullivan, had been disappeared by the death squads. The CBS crew fled the country the next day—like "migrating ducks," one journalist put it.

While the search for Bourgeois intensified, a body was found north of the capital, its face blowtorched in a death-squad custom. There was intense interest in the victim until it was determined not to be Bourgeois. Then everybody seemed to forget about the faceless man.

Bourgeois turned back up in San Salvador 10 days after he disappeared, saying he had slipped off to meet with guerrillas in the countryside, and to immerse himself in their struggle. He also released a letter stating that the "armed struggle of the Salvadoran people is justified" and "I ask the people of the United States to join with our brothers and sisters of El Salvador to do everything it can to prevent the military intervention of the United States in this country." The *Miami Herald*'s Zita Arocha was skeptical, writing that there was "speculation" that the disappearance and dramatic reappearance had all "been a ploy to gain maximum publicity." But the Maryknolls, the Catholic missionary organization of which Bourgeois belonged, which *The Washington Post* described as "one of the most radical organizations in the Catholic Church," seem to have been sincerely driven to serve in war-torn areas.

The Salvadoran government condemned Bourgeois's actions. So did journalists, since he was giving credence to government accusations that journalists all supported the guerrillas, and, as UPI correspondent Juan Tamayo wrote, "that foreign priests and nuns" all did too. In the two days after Bourgeois's reappearance, six missionaries fled the country, fearing for their safety.

In the Camino Real bar, all these fears and bravery were put on display as journalists drank hard and late. The idea was to anesthetize ourselves in order to face another day of shock and depravity. I was beginning to learn. War correspondents end up writing their colleagues' obituaries.

April 29, 1981

Salvadoran security forces were fanning out into San Salvador neighborhoods throughout the morning, locking them down, going from house to house, rounding up young men, searching for arms and contraband. At the Camino Real, it was just another day in the war. Film crews were gathering in the wide-open lobby, discussing the best options to get the "bang bang," the live war coverage that was the only film that had a chance to get on the evening news. Stateside correspondents who had "parachuted" in for some live war coverage were ready to burnish their credentials.

Gilberto showed up early, eager to get back behind the wheel of my rental car. But in the lobby of the Camino Real, we learned that the rental car lots had all been overrun with Salvadoran forces who were not letting cars in and out. We would need to spend the day "on foot," facing the heightened danger of taking taxis that would dodge security checkpoints and trigger-happy soldiers.

Steve Patten, a CBS correspondent I had met before, was in the lobby too. Steve was friendly, collaborative, and had a quick smile (none of which probably served him that well in his network career), but this morning, he was unhappy. He had been "big-footed"—the term for what happens when a big-time network correspondent shows up for a few dramatic days to earn "war correspondent" credentials. This involved grabbing the in-country cameraman and producer and leaving the real correspondent to fend for himself. In this case, that meant taking Foresta and Bullard from Patten. The big-footers rarely ventured far from the Camino Real. They would send their cameraman and producer out into the day's firefight, bombing, or street demonstration, then weave a stand-up in front of the hotel into a package that made it look like they had gone out into war. They hadn't.

Patten wanted to go out and report, but he had no camera, no crew. So he decided to join Gilberto and me. I felt like we were the Three Musketeers. Having Patten with us gave us credibility and also the experience of somebody who had been in war zones. It felt good.

The daily coverage of a Third World guerrilla war by correspondents embedded in First World hotels is like rafting a Class III rapid. You enter the day dry and helmeted. Throughout the day, you bob, weave, get thrown into rocks, and if you are lucky, you stay afloat. The current of the coverage is the waves of rumors that sometimes ripple, sometimes thunder through the lobby. On this day, they sent us on a long, hard chase.

The day, with Gilberto and Steve Patten, was a whirlwind. From a refugee camp to a press conference at the military high command.

The first wave was exciting: A guerrilla group, we heard, planned to shell the heavily fortified U.S. Embassy in the middle of San Salvador. (Later the embassy would be moved to the city's outskirts.) Despite the fact that the building had a huge brick wall surrounding it and a machine-gun nest perched atop it, this story had legs.

So did the TV correspondents. They set out in a caravan of

vans, the letters "TV" taped to front, back, and side windows, heading for the scene of the impending attack. An hour later, Gilberto, Steve, and I had caught up with the main group, all of us waiting for the "bang bang" that was expected very soon, and all settled together around sidewalk tables at Pete's, an American-style bakery directly across a busy boulevard from the embassy. Pete's was well-known in expatriate circles for its chocolate cake. Today there were piles of TV gear scattered amid the outdoor tables and chairs, and some of us went ahead and ordered dessert.

Finally, an American in a suit hustled out of the embassy entrance and hurried over to our tables. "What's going on?" he asked, eyeing the dozen or so journalists laughing and chatting in the midday heat. We had been spotted from the high-up, bulletproof windows of the embassy tower and had caused a commotion inside.

"The embassy is going to get attacked, and we're waiting to get some shots," explained one of the TV cameramen. The embassy official shook his head in total disdain and headed back to work.

As time ticked by, the journalists also began to feel the farce of the stakeout, and restlessness set in. But then there were new ripples, as the journos with phones began to get reports from their Camino Real nerve centers. Inside rooms at the hotel, Salvadoran assistants monitored police and military scanners, kept up a stream of phone calls to local officials, and tried to pick up the latest hints of military action. These guys were the eyes and ears of the correspondents, and at times the most vulnerable.

The U.S. Embassy in 1981 with new concrete walls and a pillbox on the roof. Photo by George Thurlow.

"We've got a press conference at Major," announced one journalist, referring to the Estado Mejor, the military headquarters. "Sounds like they've captured foreign mercenaries from Nicaragua with a big arms cache." That's all it took. Cameras were heaved onto shoulders, battery belts were slung like bandoliers, and soundmen scurried with bags of gear. We were rushing.

If true, the capture of Nicaraguans by the Salvadorans could set off an international crisis in Central America, where the Reagan Administration had long been accusing the Sandinistas in Nicaragua of secretly funding the Salvadoran guerrilla army. It would thoroughly discredit the Salvadoran guerrillas, who had long argued they were a home-grown army. And, though we didn't know this at the time, it would have given further ammunition to Reagan's still-secret efforts to overthrow the Nicaraguan government.

Steve, Gilberto, and I grabbed a cab to the Mejor, and when we arrived, we found the press hall abuzz with journalists from around the world. The lineup of cameras on tripods looked like the White House briefing room. This, I thought, was going to be a big one.

Two disheveled Nicaraguans were soon marched to a long, narrow table, and the feeding frenzy began. Gilberto offered the translations, and though I couldn't tell if he was really keeping up with the fast-paced interview, I did understand that things were going downhill fast.

The two men explained they were Nicaraguan fishermen and had come across the bay between the two countries in a small rowboat. They were in shock at all the cameras and lights. When reporters asked them why they came, they said it was to get away from the Sandinistas, not to fight the Salvadoran army. They were poor, they explained, and figured life would be better in El Salvador.

You could feel the air sucked out of the room. Camera lights were quickly killed, even as the Salvadoran military minders kept up their chatter about how the two men were likely to have been guerrilla sympathizers. It didn't work. Cameras were being pulled from their mounts. Reporters were beginning to drift out of the room. You could taste the disappointment, though part of me liked the rush of watching big media be taken for a ride. The TV press corps were so easily swung from one end of town to another, chasing anything that might have a chance on the evening news, eagerly hoping for a "hero gram," the rare pat on the back from network executives in New York.

Gilberto, Steve, and I quickly had a more pressing problem. While everybody else climbed back into their "TV-tattooed" minivans, we needed a way to get back into town. We tried to catch a cab out in front of the military headquarters. No luck: No cabbie in his right mind was going to pick up three guys standing out in front of the most notorious hub of violent repression. And behind us, uniformed kids in their teens, lugging big rifles, were starting to look at us like we were enemy combatants who had snuck into their fort.

When a minivan filled with a Salvadoran TV crew pulled up and offered to ferry us back to the Camino Real, we gladly accepted. We were safe, given help by the locals. The minivan, like others I had seen, was not luxurious. It had been stripped of any comfort or convenience and was filled with bulky cameras, spare battery belts, and long coils of audio wires. This crew worked for the government TV station, and on the dashboard, they had installed a police/military scanner. As I spotted the Camino Real looming in the distance, the chatter in the front seat intensified. The radio was reporting fighting in Soyapango.

Soyapango, a gritty suburb about 10 kilometers from the hotel, was home to working-class Salvadorans who labored in nearby factories and mills. It was also a hotbed of rebellion, the site of the clandestine headquarters of one of the FMLN guerrilla groups, as well as the Agua Caliente power plant, which was critical to providing electricity to many of the local industries. The guerrilla groups would sometimes attack the plant as part of a campaign to bring down infrastructure, damage the economy, and weaken the government. The area had already been bombed by Salvadoran Air Force jets provided by the U.S. Rarely had bombing been carried out in an urban area, but Soyapango was considered the guerrilla dagger poised at the heart of San Salvador.

Soyapango also had a garrison of Treasury Police, or the Policía de Hacienda, formed in 1926 by the government to thwart smuggling, illegal liquor brewing, and tax evasion. As the civil war heated up, the Treasury Police had been transformed into a 2,000-member urban war machine with a dismal record on human rights. Former State Department official Elliott Abrams said the Treasury Police were at one time "among the most notorious abusers of human rights in El Salvador." In his book *The Protection Racket State*, William Stanley concluded they were "the principal violator of human rights in the second half of the 1980s," with a strategy of "mass murder." Even the U.S. Immigration and Naturalization Service (INS) noted that in the early 1980s, the Treasury Police "had the reputation as the most ruthless and brutal of the three security forces." Like the other government security organizations, including the National Guard and the regular army, the Treasury Police formed an intelligence unit, S-II, that worked closely with death squads in kidnapping and "disappearing" civilians and suspected guerrilla sympathizers. The Salvadoran government attempted to address concerns in the U.S. Congress with human rights abuses by disbanding these intelligence units, including those in the Treasury Police. By 1987 and 1988, however, the U.S. government noted that the Treasury Police were "implicated in a resurgence of death squad activity." The INS report revealed that some members of the U.S. diplomatic corps referred to them as "Gestapo." They were composed, wrote Shirley Christian in *The Atlantic*, of "the toughest, meanest men in villages and rural townships" who had served in the Army and now "were offered lifetime careers" roughing people up. Juan Tamayo, the UPI Mexico City bureau chief who regularly reported from San Salvador, said the Treasury Police were the "boogeymen. If you ran into a Treasury Police checkpoint at night, that was when you got worried. They had a reputation as being the worst."

On April 7, 1981, three weeks before my arrival in San Salvador, the Treasury Police had carried out a massacre in Soyapango. Twenty-three young men and women had been killed, and while the government originally indicated the deaths occurred in a ferocious firefight, the first journalists on the scene found the victims with gunshot wounds to the head and some with their hands tied behind their backs. One male victim had been castrated and his penis left on his chest.

As with so many incidents in El Salvador during the dirty war years, what happened in the early morning hours of April 7 is not altogether clear. According to Col. Francisco Antonio Moran, 20 of his men had been dispatched to house No. 16 on Calle Principal to break up a "terrorist cell" at that address. Moran claimed that his men met "heavy gunfire" from the house and his unit was repulsed after killing 23 men, women, and teens. The Treasury Police reported that after their men retreated from the scene, the "terrorists" had mutilated the bodies to "mislead public opinion."

The right-wing *News-Gazette*, an English-language weekly owned by a notorious death-squad supporter, said neighbors had never seen the 23 who were killed before, suggesting that they were guerrilla interlopers. But other newspapers said two of those killed had owned a local *pupuseria*, and the reporting in *The New York Times* suggesting a horrifying picture, with people being pulled from No. 16 and executed on the street.

The Catholic Church's Socorro Juridico, a human rights organization based in San Salvador, had more details. It reported that the 20 Treasury Police were accompanied by two men wearing masks who pointed out the homes where people were to be captured. Socorro Juridico's official report of the incident quoted family members of the victims, who said their loved ones had all been in their homes sleeping. Socorro Juridico also noted that the arrests came during the martial law curfew and many of those arrested had their thumbs tied together, a common security force procedure. Later, Socorro Juridico asserted, those captured were executed by the Treasury Police, including a 48-year-old worker, a 17-year-old female maid, and several teenaged students. The youngest executed was 13.

Officials in Washington were skeptical of the Treasury Police report. State Department spokesman William J. Dyess declared that the shooting was a "tragic event." Liberal U.S. senators, led by Edward Kennedy, used the event to fan anti-war flames in Washington, and Kennedy called for an end to U.S. military aid to El Salvador.

In response to pressure from Washington, the Salvadoran government fired 59 Treasury Police officers a few days after the incident. As more pressure mounted, Col. Moran changed his tune, quoted by the *Times* as saying some of his officers might face criminal charges as a result of the shootings.

Much of that was still unfolding when we entered Soyapango, but we had seen the photographs of those young, slaughtered Salvadorans, laid out in neat rows. I assumed that the news coming through the police radio must be of yet another massacre. We should head to Soyapango to document it, I said. Steve agreed. Gilberto was ready for action. The Salvadoran TV crew was all in. This was their bread and butter. We passed the Camino Real and headed for the bang bang.

The scene upon our arrival at 4:45 p.m. on a busy street in Soyapango was both surreal and familiar. A long line of TV minivans had pulled to the side of a busy thoroughfare.

Soldiers were everywhere, crouching and running. Every now and then, a shot went whizzing by. In the distance, more gunshots. This did not seem to be a massacre after all. It was a firefight. We were told by a TV reporter that the shooting was coming from the Agua Caliente power plant, ahead of us at the bottom of the canyon, as the guerrillas tried to shut it down and the military tried to stop them.

Ahead of us, the NBC crew was crouching behind a wall, try-

The Agua Caliente power plant. Photo by George Thurlow.

ing to determine where the fighting was going on. As we hung
low behind the Salvadoran minivan, two other TV minivans
roared past and turned down the power plant road. "Hey, there
go my guys," Patten said, pointing to the occupants of one of
the minivans. "Let's follow them down the road."

We looked at the Salvadoran TV crews. They weren't budging.
We should have stuck with the locals, but we were there for the
bang bang. There were gunshots all around us, and Steve had
an opportunity to file a report with his crew. We took off.

Even though bullets whizzed by, normal vehicle traffic came
and went at the intersection. As we walked down power plant
raod, there was nobody to be seen. Suddenly, on our right, a
man edged out from between two shacks and motioned to us.
"Stay down" was what his hands told us. Instead, we continued on our way.

The scene near the Agua Caliente power plant just before the journalists were shot. A crew from NBC news can be seen in the distance. Photo by George Thurlow.

About 100 meters down the road, the houses disappeared and there was jungle on one side of the road, where where a stream ran through town. On the other side, a tall cliff rose to another part of the Soyapango neighborhood.

There was no sign of the TV crews. But at that moment, from around a curve, Associated Press photographer Joaquin Zuniga came walking toward us.

"Where are the others?" Gilberto asked.

"Just down around the curve," Zuniga answered.

"Is it safe?" Gilberto asked.

"Yes, just keep down," was Zuniga's reply.

We were now in the middle of the street. There was no traffic, no people. The gunshots sounded closer. Occasionally there was the whine of a bullet.

I was carrying my battered Konica 35 mm camera—not exactly war correspondent gear. I had probably shot 10 frames. Gilberto was carrying our tape recorders, notebooks, and water in a plastic grocery bag.

As the gunshots seemed to pick up, Steve turned to Gilberto and asked for his tape recorder. He was ready to do an actuality, a live report from a war zone explaining what was happening, with the gunshots providing the realistic backdrop. Gilberto stopped to bend over and take out the tape recorder, and gunshots exploded in the street all around us.

Instinctively I moved toward the cliff, and as the shots intensified and began hitting the road around us, I dived into a small culvert. It was no more than eight inches deep. I looked toward Gilberto and saw him stumble. Blood came shooting out of his mouth, and he fell.

Steve turned and ran back up the road. An NBC cameraman caught him, yelling, "The guy's dead. Get your ass over here."

I don't remember hearing him. The gunshots continued, and suddenly, I felt a sharp pain up and down my left arm. I had been hit. My hand, elbow, and shoulder were bleeding. I had one clear thought: *Stay on the ground in the culvert and you are dead. Get up and run.*

I ran.

I don't remember where the gunshots came from then—just

that I took off down the power plant road, toward the curve where the other journalists were, and that as I rounded it, I saw a military truck with a soldier crouched behind it. On the side of the road, a half-dozen Salvadoran journalists were hunkered down. Blood was streaming from numerous shrapnel wounds in my arm, and they turned their cameras toward me.

I was becoming the news. I was the bang bang. That night, my image would flash across the U.S. on network TV, and I would be heralded, pitied, and pilloried. I was, depending on how you saw it, a heroic journalist trying to uncover the truth about our dirty little war in El Salvador, a fool for stumbling around in the middle of a firefight, and a symbol of American arrogance abroad. Like my country, I was blundering opportunistically forward, with my actions resulting in tragedy for others.

In true war-zone dark humor, a Salvadoran journalist ran up and said to me, "What's the matter, buddy?" Someone used a microphone cord to tie a makeshift tourniquet to slow the bleeding in my hand and elbow. Someone else got on his phone and tried to call the Camino Real on my behalf. There was no answer. My bloody, handwritten notes indicate it was 5:15 p.m.

Salvadoran TV journalists tend to Thurlow's wounds in Agua Caliente. A screenshot from NBC nightly news April 29, 1981.

Within minutes, from the distance came the sweet sound of sirens. The heroic drivers and attendants of the Green Cross were the only ones who ventured into shooting zones to rescue the wounded and dying. I was escorted into their ambulance, and we headed back up the road.

That night, on the NBC *Nightly News*, correspondent Jim Cummins aired footage of the shooting, Gilberto's body, and the rush to get me into an ambulance. His final words: "Most witnesses say maybe the journalists were mistaken for guerrillas. Maybe not." The suggestion, it seemed, was that this may have been a deliberate attack, part of what was becoming open season on journalists.

The door was rolled open as we passed Gilberto's body, face up, beside the road. Nobody was near him, and we all assumed he was dead. There were flies on his face and a large stain on his crotch. A few words were exchanged between the ambulance crew and the bystanders, the door was closed, and the ambulance roared off toward the Policlínica San Salvador, an upscale hospital used by Americans seeking the best medical treatment.

Later, I was told they found my business card in Gilberto's pocket, with a bullet hole clean through it. Years after that, I saw photos of his body being tossed into the back of a military truck, the kind used for hauling civilian bodies and kidnapped detainees.

For now, though, I was shuttled off to the hospital, where I sat outside the operating room, waiting for the surgeon and worrying about whether I'd have permanent damage in my arm. UPI's San Salvador bureau chief John Newhagen snapped a photo of me in a white T-shirt, blood smeared over my left arm. Twenty years later, when I asked him about the shot, which was sent on the UPI all over the world, he said he did not remember it. "I shot a lot of bodies," he recalled. My body did not stand out.

It was unsettling to be wheeled into the operating room, its antiquated equipment and mental-hospital-green walls a reminder that even in the best clinic in El Salvador, I was still in the middle of the poorest country in the hemisphere.

The surgeon pulled several pieces of twisted metal from my hand. Years later, when I showed the shrapnel to a military veteran, he said it looked like anti-personnel shrapnel that is packed into a shotgun shell, and that it can be devastating at close range. The surgeon elected not to dig the shrapnel pieces, one as big as a nickel, out of my elbow and shoulder.

When I awoke from the anesthesia, I was in a hospital room with some shady-looking characters hovering around my bed. A translator explained that they were security officers from the military there to interview me. I did my best to explain that I had no idea where the firing had come from. They told me that Patten, Moran, and I had wandered into a firefight between the military and the guerrillas, and that we had foolishly kept going when we should have turned back.

To my great relief, Steve Patten arrived at the hospital later on, safe and unharmed. But he had a different story of the shooting. He told me that Joaquin Zuniga was also in the hospital. (The UPI also sent a photo around the world of him being hustled from a second ambulance.)

Zuniga, Patten said, told fellow journalists that he had passed us, motioned us toward the larger group of journalists, and then noticed soldiers above us. He pointed his camera at them, and as he did so, they opened fire on him and us. Zuniga was hit in the thigh. His injuries were serious, the bullet nicking his sciatic nerve.

Zuniga's story belied the official version. We had been shot from above by soldiers and, as it turned out, they were worst of the worst, the Treasury Police.

While my personal integrity had been restored, my personal safety was now at risk: I was an embarrassment to the Salvadoran government. Their soldiers had opened fire on an American journalist, killing his driver and seriously wounding a UPI photographer. As I lay in the hospital that night and the next day, it was clear that I needed to get out of El Salvador. Several journalists told me that they worried that I, like John Sullivan and—as we thought at the time—Father Roy Bourgeois, could be disappeared.

So I was grateful when Todd Greentree, then vice consul of the U.S. Embassy, came to see me in the hospital. It was reassuring to know that the Embassy knew of my whereabouts. It made me feel less worried that I would disappear on the military-controlled road to the airport—the same place four American churchwomen had been kidnapped, raped, and killed.

When I was released from the hospital, I went back to the Camino Real. I was heavily bandaged and suffering from hospital-induced dysentery.

Gilberto Moran's young wife and baby came there too, hoping that the journalists, including me, would collect money to pay for Gilberto's funeral and their living expenses. I scraped up what I had left, and Steve did the same. In all, some $600 was handed over.

"Yeah," said one journalist at the hotel that day. "I've had several drivers shot out from under me." This was the bravado of the press corps, but also the callousness toward the Salvadorans that kept them out of harm's way. It struck me as the worst kind of bragging.

I should have tried to do more for Gilberto's family, but I didn't. I felt isolated, guilty in a way I didn't know how to handle, and frightened. I took the cowardly route. As I recall, I didn't even show up to the hotel lobby to meet Gilberto's wife face-to-face.

Rosa Lillia, the young nun I had met a few days before at the orphanage, also came to see me at the hotel. When the call came from the lobby, I did go down to say goodbye. She handed me a small medallion and a note written on the back of a postcard of the Government Palace, a place of deep evil. It read, "*Jorge, que la experiencia que visitiste en este país, sea un testimorio más de la represión y violencia que me pueblo. Tu amiga, Rosa Lillia.*" (Translation: "From your experience, from your visit in this country, you have much evidence of the repression and violence against my people. Your friend, Rosa Lillia.") She fled El Salvador soon after I'd flown home.

I remember several TV journalists agreeing to drive with me to the airport the next morning. Published accounts indicate I was also accompanied by two Embassy security guards, as a result of pressure from both the offices of California Senator Alan Cranston and local elected officials in Santa Barbara.

The doctors had said I needed to have specialists look at my arm to ensure I would not lose use of my shoulder or elbow. I knew I'd be taken care of in the U.S. and would have a story unlike any I had ever written. But Gilberto Moran's family was being abandoned.

Like President Reagan, and like so many other Americans, I had come to El Salvador to make a point, and I was leaving behind a trail of misery. I had stories to tell, anti-war speeches to make, and a clear understanding of how the U.S. was behind so much of the terror. But it would take me 20 years to figure out my responsibility. My country never has.

Aftermath

Upon my return, there was a whirlwind of writing and talking: People wanted my firsthand account of the shooting. Sacramento TV stations interviewed me. Anti-war groups had me on their programs. The Woodland paper ran my five-part series, and I was glad that only one article dealt with the shooting. The rest described a U.S.-backed terror campaign against the people of El Salvador.

The day after the shooting, Congressmember Vic Fazio, who represented Woodland, had sent a letter to U.S. Secretary of State Alexander Haig, calling for an investigation of the shooting to begin "as soon as possible." In a later letter to his

Congressional colleagues that contained my reporting for the *Daily Democrat*, Fazio offered the articles as "another element in the growing pool of evidence which suggests that the Administration's policy toward El Salvador suffers from serious inherent flaws."

The U.S. Embassy also contacted the State Department after the shooting, sending a cable saying that, despite witness accounts of government soldiers shooting, Embassy staff could not determine the source confidently themselves.

But the State Department—and the Salvadoran military— declined to initiate investigations of the shooting. State Department spokesperson Mayer Nudell said she did not think an investigation was in order. It was, she said, "not unusual for even the most seasoned journalist to get into the situation" of stumbling into a crossfire. Perhaps this was kind of her: The original cable had contained a "confidential" portion that implied I and the others suffered from "inexperience."

As I became the subject of the news I'd meant to cover from the sidelines, other people pointed to my inexperience in more public venues.

On May 23, 1981, Juan Tamayo, the UPI international bureau chief, sent a piece across the world headlined "Freelance Journalists Brave Dangers but Are Inexperienced." His examples of freelancers who showed up in El Salvador included an Italian literature professor from UC Berkeley, "a Norwegian beauty who wears skin-tight jump suits," the son of a former British ambassador, three college students from Arizona State looking for part-time work, and me.

He quoted one regular journalist in El Salvador saying, "The fastest ticket to a bodybag is an inexperienced freelancer. They think it's a *Kojak* show and they can scream 'cut' when it gets heavy."

"Most of the freelancers are inexperienced but serious about their work," Tamayo wrote. "But others are irresponsible romantics who take foolish risks with their lives—and too often those of others—for little more than 'kicks.'" A landscape architect who worked as an Aspen ski photographer and then showed up in El Salvador to shoot the war, for example, routinely made drunken dashes from the hotel bar to his nearby apartment, despite a shoot-to-kill curfew that had claimed 800 violators since early 1981. Then came the zinger: "Not so lucky was George Thurlow, 28, a reporter for the Woodland, Calif., *Daily Democrat* wounded April 29, four days after his arrival, by police who mistook him for a guerrilla during a firefight.

"Thurlow's $25-a-day Salvadoran translator ... was killed in the gunbattle, leaving behind a wife, a 3-year-old child and a whopping funeral bill.

"Thurlow approached the firefight through an exposed route, according to witnesses, and wrote a story—after he left El Salvador—saying Salvadoran police 'shoot first and don't ask questions later.'"

(My comment was used by Salvadoran military officers who used it to justify their hostility toward the foreign press and their charges that the media was helping the guerrillas.)

Tamayo went on: "Told that fellow journalists were criticizing his trip ... Thurlow said, 'I am ready for criticism that I deserve. I am willing to take the criticism. I've got a guy's life on my head.'" I was glad that he ran my admission, but it didn't protect me from the truth of his indictment.

Tamayo's piece was run in both the *Miami Herald* and, two months later, *Quill*, the official publication of the Society of Professional Journalists. And no wonder: He had a point, particularly the sharp needle about paying Gilberto $25 a day, then a princely sum in El Salvador, but something like slave wages when you consider the risk and consequences.

A few weeks before Tamayo's piece, and just days after my shooting, *The New York Times* had carried an Associated Press dispatch noting that the Salvadoran military was banning journalists from areas of military action. My case was clearly being used to punish all journalists and keep them from the war zones. "The announcement," said the AP, "was included in a communique yesterday in which the military expressed sorrow over the death of a Salvadoran interpreter and the wounds suffered by two journalists, one a United States citizen, during an army sweep of an area attacked by leftist guerrillas." The AP tossed in its own barb. Despite the fact that the item ran just three paragraphs, it noted that I had been on a "working vacation." There was no better way to demonstrate just how pathetic my actions had been.

The military ban didn't last long, but the bitterness felt by the "pros" in El Salvador did. For one thing, they were constricted by the fact that there were death lists and threats routinely aimed at journalists. The military leadership repeatedly indicated that they felt the foreign media, meaning U.S. media, were sympathetic to the leftist movement and anti-military. It is true that American journalists were shocked by the brutality of the military and its death squads, and with good reason. Correspondents dreaded receiving "the letter" from a death squad or far-right businessmen, warning them to leave El Salvador for what was seen as overly sympathetic reporting on leftists. This was one reason why, as Mattison had put it to me in the bar, "It's better to have the umbrella of the right and flirt with the left."

It was freelancers, I was convinced, who could come in, write the truth about El Salvador, and then leave before they suffered the retributions of the military. The pros were constrained and endured self-censorship. Freelancers had the freedom to ask questions, stick their nose where it was not welcome, and then leave the country and report exactly what they saw and heard.

As the months went by, I was still outraged about the war in El Salvador, and still feeling guilty about my role in Gilberto Moran's death. By December 1981, I had become the editor of the alternative newspaper in Northern California the *Chico News & Review*. But I still felt that the Reagan Administration was giving free rein to the Salvadoran military and its death squads, and perhaps some part of me still yearned to be a respected foreign correspondent. So, I opted to spend Christmas that year not with family or friends, but in Mexico City, where, in a small, cramped apartment, I sat at the feet of the legendary Salvadoran journalist and publisher Jorge Pinto.

Like many liberal and leftist leaders in Latin America, Pinto came from a family of aristocrats. His family had begun making newspapers in El Salvador in the 1800s, a power that gave them wealth and privilege. His grandfather founded the daily

Siglo Veinte (*Twentieth Century*). His independent-minded father continued the tradition with *Diario Latino*, where his editorials, critical of the government, briefly landed him in jail.

In 1955, Pinto had opened *El Independiente* (*The Independent*). It published until January 16, 1981, when army troops arrested his staff and smashed his editorial equipment as he was cabling a story to the *Los Angeles Times*. His criticism of the government and the military ended his journalism career. He fled almost immediately to Mexico.

Chain-smoking as he watched Christmas Day revelers on the Mexico City streets below, Pinto lamented the lack of press freedom in El Salvador. The Reagan Administration was trumpeting the value of elections that were to be held in March 1982, but, Pinto said, "We have press people in jail. It is absolutely ridiculous to talk about elections." How could there be free elections in the middle of a civil war, when most opponents of the government had been either killed or driven from the country? "To make journalism in our country is a dangerous thing," Pinto continued. If he returned to start a newspaper that supported opponents of the government, "they would kill us."

One of the last warnings that Pinto issued that Christmas Day was, "We are going to have a country for all, or we are going to have a country for nobody."

At the time, the Salvadoran government was officially headed by President Jose Napoleon Duarte, but for all intents and purposes, it was controlled by the military high commander, Gen. Jose Guillermo Garcia. At the nearby Mexico City offices of the Salvadoran Catholic Church's Legal Aid, Roberto

Cuellar kept a weekly report of those who had been kidnapped or killed by either the military or the guerrillas. More than 90 percent of the reports allege military or death-squad responsibility.

Cuellar had fled El Salvador after his house was shot up and he received repeated death threats. One of Cuellar's most recent reports out of Mexico City had caught my attention: Dr. Carlos Armando Vargas, 31, a second-generation Salvadoran physician, had been grabbed on December 16, 1981, after stepping out of his clinic, a clinic his father had founded in downtown San Salvador. Vargas had been the general secretary of the Committee for the Defense of El Salvador Patients, a group of physicians that had protested military intrusions into hospitals and the kidnapping of patients. His picture and that of other members of the Committee had recently appeared in a local San Salvador newspaper.

Witnesses said a group of gun-toting, civilian-clad men had been outside the clinic and apparently were not questioned by a military patrol that had passed them earlier. When one man in the group pointed out Vargas and Vargas resisted, he was then grabbed, hit, and thrown into a nearby vehicle that fled the scene. Despite U.S. inquiries into his welfare, Vargas was never seen again, though his family received unofficial reports that he had been held in a National Guard jail.

Cuellar explained that he had contacted Vargas's sister, Evelyn Castaneda, who was married to a physicist and lived in Davis, California. This was just outside my old turf in Woodland, and not far from where I was currently working at the *Chico News & Review*. When I returned from Mexico City that

Christmas, I tracked down Evelyn Castaneda, and she agreed to be interviewed. My interview and a sidebar on Pinto and Cuellar appeared soon after in *The Sacramento Bee* and the *Chico News & Review.*

Castaneda and her family called the U.S. State Department and several representatives of Congress to enlist their help in obtaining Vargas's release. According to Castaneda, her sister, then living in Belmont, California, had received a call from a State Department official in late December 1981 confirming that Vargas was alive and that the U.S. government would keep the family informed about his condition. Family members in El Salvador were told by the U.S. Embassy that they would investigate the kidnapping.

The kidnapping of physicians in El Salvador was not unusual. The military accused many physicians of secretly giving medical treatment to guerrillas. They were also targeted by death squads because they were part of El Salvador's intellectual class.

While I was being treated for my gunshot wounds in 1981 at the Policlínica in downtown San Salvador, I was told that a doctor had been abducted from the steps of the clinic just days before. Ironically, when asked about security at the Policlínica, a U.S. Embassy official told me it was one of the safest places in San Salvador because it was "within the security net placed around the U.S. Embassy."

My article in *The Sacramento Bee* and the family's determination to find their brother and win his release spurred action. Liberal U.S. Representative Vic Fazio wrote to Salvadoran President Jose Napoleon Duarte and asked that Vargas be released from custody. "We have reason to believe that he is currently being held in a jail run by your National Guard. His only 'offense' has been to protest recent military attacks on patients who were being treated in area hospitals." The letter was signed by 51 members of the House of Representatives, among them many who would try to end U.S. support for the war in El Salvador throughout the rest of the decade.

In a fit of journalistic outrage and impropriety, I wrote a letter on *Chico News & Review* letterhead to conservative Republican Congressmember Gene Chappie, who represented Chico. "As both an editor and a constituent I would like to ask your help in clarifying just what Dr. Vargas's status is, what role the U.S. State Department is playing in this situation, and why such human rights abuses as this are continuing at a time the Reagan Administration contends they are on decline," I wrote.

It was a critical time for the Salvadoran military. Congress was on the verge of approving a huge increase in military aid to El Salvador even as the Reagan Administration gave the Salvadoran government a thumbs-up on human rights.

Congressmember Fazio had sponsored a resolution to cut off all military aid to El Salvador unless the "government makes a serious effort to end generally recognized human rights violations." Chappie responded to my brazen letter by noting that he had sent a letter to Secretary of State Alexander Haig, "asking his assistance in locating Dr. Carlos Vargas. I have asked Secretary [of State Alexander] Haig's office to keep me informed of any information they can gain. Given the turbulent political situation in El Salvador now, I must tell you that it may be a difficult task to locate Dr. Vargas."

The wording was ominous, but there were many jails in El Salvador, and killing a doctor with connections in the U.S. would be the height of military arrogance.

Twenty-four years later, as I examined and reexamined my notes and files on El Salvador, I came across my *Bee* article and that letter to Rep. Chappie.

I had long ago quit the foreign war beat. My friend Jeff von Kaenel, who had convinced me to start working at the *Santa Barbara News & Review* in the 1970s, cut a deal with the owners of the *Chico News & Review* in the early 1980s: He would take over the paper and bring it back from the precipice of bankruptcy. He offered me equity in the paper if I would take over as editor. The entire editorial staff quit in protest of my hiring; they questioned my politics, and whether I would merely be a puppet for Jeff's schemes. So, I built a staff from scratch, and with them, I helped to rebuild what became an award-winning paper I had become proud of.

Now, I was taking stock of the past. What had happened to Dr. Vargas? Maybe he had been found, I thought. Maybe there was a happy story to tell. In March 2005, I called Evelyn Castaneda, her physicist husband easily found through Google. (I would have never found her had I not noted her connection to him and his research work at UC Davis. I'd left that information in the original story to help her be seen as credible at a time when anybody accusing the Salvadoran government of crimes was quickly labeled a guerrilla or a leftist.) After identifying myself on the phone and reminding her of the *Bee* story, I asked, "Did you ever find your brother?"

"No," she said softly. "Nothing."

I could not let it go at that. I wanted closure, so while taking my family on a spring break vacation at Lake Tahoe, I called and asked to meet with Evelyn. She quickly agreed, and we met in the library of the private girls' Catholic school in Sacramento where she had been a Spanish teacher for the past 14 years.

The story was complicated, and at least twice, Evelyn started to cry. First, when she talked of her brother, and later when she talked about the people of El Salvador. She related how she and her brother had grown up in the affluence of a middle-class family, in a large house in San Salvador. But when her father had died, her brother had been forced to take over his clinic and her mother took in boarders to help make ends meet.

Her brother Carlos had attended the University of El Salvador medical school, at a time when the university was a hotbed of student revolt against the repressive military dictatorship. Their father was a medical technician who opened a clinical laboratory in the capital. It was located on 11 Avenue North in downtown San Salvador and called Laboratoria Pasteur. When their father died in 1980, Carlos took over running the laboratory.

Carlos was different from his conservative businessman father. "He always had compassion for the people. As a 17-year-old, he ended up at Rosales Hospital after a motorcycle crash. He had no connections and no identification, but he realized his fortunate status waiting in a gurney at the public hospital."

Rosales had always been a hospital for the poor, and its conditions have long been among the worst in El Salvador. His sensitivity to the poor, his exposure to radicalism at the university, and his own idealism eventually led Carlos to work with other physicians to help the poor.

Evelyn related a simple but telling story of his experience. During his internship, Carlos had been working in a maternity hospital. A young woman came in to deliver a child and Carlos was the attending physician. The woman wanted to assume the childbirth position that generations of indigenous people had passed to their women: Squatting is the most natural and quickest way to deliver a baby. But the nurses refused to let her get out of bed. "Carlos came and talked to her, and she told him, 'I know how to do this.' He later told me, 'They [the poor] know more than we do.'"

As she told the story, Evelyn's eyes welled up. "He believed in people being in charge of their well-being."

After his disappearance, Evelyn found out that her brother had also been helping out "with a clinic run by nuns in San Salvador. He was reserved; he was not outspoken," she recalled. But he was also an officer in a physicians' group, the Committee for the Defense of El Salvador Patients, which had criticized the military's practice of entering hospitals and grabbing patients who then disappeared.

After the *Bee* article appeared and the group of Congressmembers sent a demanding letter to the Reagan Administration, Evelyn held out hope her brother would be found. Now, 24 years later, she admitted, "I don't think we learned anything."

There was an incident involving the students who lived at her mother's house. Four years after Carlos had disappeared, the police came and arrested all the roomers. They accused them of having knowledge of the kidnapping of President Duarte's daughter. Even Evelyn's mother was placed under arrest, though a day later she was released. That came only after the Salvadoran Archbishop intervened with government officials.

"There was one man they never released," she recalled. "He just disappeared. His name was Alejandro Vazquez, and he was a public accountant. He disappeared."

I asked Evelyn if she had made peace with both the Salvadoran government and its American backers.

Her reply was thoughtful and sophisticated. "There are so many decent people here in [American] society, and still, if they are not given the truth with graphic pictures, they are not going to go look for it. It is uncomfortable to learn that your government might be doing things in your name that you do not approve."

I pressed her on whether the U.S. government, which backed the Salvadoran military and security forces and was implicated in the death squad's operation, bore some responsibility for her brother's disappearance. "I hold the U.S. government responsible," she flatly said. "There were others involved, but government people have got responsibilities. They collaborated knowingly with the assassins."

Why, though, would the men of El Salvador do this to each other? "Maybe the Salvadorans wanted to identify with the powerful brothers to the north and wanted to do their bidding.

That is the only explanation I have. Maybe the powerful in the U.S. know how to manipulate fears, use those fears of people, to their own advantage."

I asked Evelyn if she intended to return to El Salvador and continue the search for her brother. She teared up again and said, "No." At this point, she knew there was no point in hoping he might be alive. It was too painful seeing the suffering of her people. She would not return.

A few months later, after a series of phone calls and emails, I met Evelyn's other, living brother, Ernesto Vargas, in the lobby of the Camino Real hotel. Ernesto Vargas was 50 and worked as a computer technician in San Salvador. He was vague about his actions at the time of his brother's disappearance, saying simply, "I was in a bad way in those days." His sister-in-law had come to his house on December 17, 1981, and told him, "They got [Carlos]."

Ernesto had more specifics about the kidnapping. Carlos had left the clinic to go Christmas shopping, he said. "There were two cars. A minibus, and the other was a Toyota pickup. When Carlos left the clinic, they grabbed him and put him in the back of the pickup. These two cars did not have licenses, and while they had been parked near the clinic, a truck full of National Guard soldiers had driven by. Somebody later told me the soldiers just passed by and said nothing. They knew these people."

At the time, Ernesto had one connection to a person in President Duarte's family. He called his contact and told him about Carlos's kidnapping. "I didn't mention the cars, but this person asked me if there were two cars involved. When I said 'Yes,' he responded, 'I'm sorry. There is nothing I can do.'"

Ernesto said the Treasury Police had custody of Carlos initially but admitted that was only a rumor. He was also more open about why Carlos may have been a target. "After he disappeared, we searched through his things. We found an organizational chart. There were two or three boxes, and one had his name. One of the boarders in my mother's house told me years later that my brother was in charge of caring for people in the guerrilla hospitals."

Where, I asked indelicately, could his body be?

"In those days, they took people and dumped them in El Playón, a place where vultures ate the flesh off the bones of the death squad victims." Maybe vultures or dogs had eaten his brother's body, he said.

El Salvador is better off now, Ernesto asserted. "We don't have military forces killing people or making them disappear. They had that power. They don't anymore. But the same people that were behind the military power still have the power. They won't let our economic situation change."

I asked about what it would mean to seek justice for his brother. If he knew their names, he would try to bring the kidnappers and killers to justice. But he has no clues, and after 24 years, nobody in El Salvador has come to him and given him even the slightest bit of information about what happened to his brother in December 1981.

"What I would really like is for the truth to be known and

these people apologize," Ernesto said. "I don't want them to go to jail. They were part of a big war. They were taken over by this wave of violence."

When I talked with Ernesto, I was in El Salvador hoping to advance some form of justice on my own. For years, I had kept myself from truly looking back. But on the eve of 2000, I had admitted to myself that my own actions had been paltry, and I decided to return to El Salvador, track down Gilberto Moran's grave, and find his wife and child. It would be emotional—humiliating, I assumed, and uncomfortable—but maybe I could try to make amends, listen to how Gilberto's death had marked his child's life, put the by-then young adult through college. My country has a habit of entering other countries, leaving devastation and orphans in its wake, and conveniently forgetting its actions. I couldn't change U.S. foreign policy, but I could at least try to act differently myself.

My first trip back turned into a 25-year journey, worth every tortuous step, with repeat visits to El Salvador as well as trips across the U.S. to learn from friends and colleagues. The name Moran is as familiar in El Salvador as the name Johnson is in the United States, and I have yet to find Gilberto Moran's grave, or his family. But I have tried to reckon with the truth, and to tender some form of apology of my own. I am still figuring out how. The least I can do is show the American culpability in all this violence. I want to chronicle the brave Americans and Salvadorans who stood up to the thugs in Washington and San Salvador. I want to remind America that our adventures in other places leave behind deep scars. And I want to remind myself that I owe a debt that has yet to be repaid.

Part II

The Firemen

From my perch at the paper in Chico, where I worked as editor from 1981 to 1991, I had watched other journalists in Central America, and the people who worked with them, suffer. On June 21, 1983, Dial Torgerson, the legendary reporter I'd admired and been excited just to be near at the Camino Real, was killed. Torgerson was heading back from covering fighting along the Honduras–Nicaragua border, and his car hit a land mine on a road used by Contras, based in Honduras, for attacks inside Nicaragua. Also in the car, and also killed, was Richard Cross, a 33-year-old freelance writer who just three days earlier had been hired for an assignment by *U.S. News & World Report*. He had previously worked as a freelance photographer in El Salvador. Severely wounded was their driver, Jose Herrero, who died later from his wounds.

Torgerson was among at least a dozen Americans killed and wounded covering Central American wars in the 1980s and 1990s. Dozens of Salvadoran journalists were also killed.

And drivers, men like Jose Herrero and Gilberto Moran, were treated as afterthoughts, if at all, in coverage of the war dead. They were the unsung and largely unremembered heroes of our quest for truth.

At the time of Torgerson's death, the U.S. government was running a secret war against Nicaragua's Sandinista government. In an attempt to discredit the Sandinistas, the U.S. government falsely asserted that Torgerson had been killed by a grenade launched by Nicaraguan government troops. U.S. Embassy spokesperson Robert Callahan had told reporters that the grenade had "utterly destroyed their car." He was further quoted as saying, "The impact of the shell drove the car about three to four feet in the air.... They [Nicaraguan soldiers] opened fire with machine guns."

Only after a team of journalists traveled to the site and discovered a deep crater in the road, and all the evidence of a land mine, was the American Embassy report discredited.

(Many years later, Lynda Schuster, herself a foreign correspondent who covered Latin America, would write a love letter to Torgerson, whom she had married just 10 months before he died. It appeared in the Cuban newspaper *Granma*, but later was reprinted in the *Utne Reader*, and describes a frantic love affair between two correspondents who were rarely together, each often flying off to dangerous locations because, Schuster wrote, "Everything is dictated by the story." This was what fed the romanticism of being a foreign correspondent. Love and danger were an intoxicating brew.)

It does not appear that Torgerson and Cross were actually targeted for killing, but for other journalists who died on the job, there is plenty of evidence that Salvadoran soldiers considered foreign reporters fair game, since the high command saw most of them as guerrilla sympathizers.

John Hoagland may have been one of them. A photojournalist who some say was the inspiration for the movie *Under Fire*, Hoagland had covered one hot spot after another in a career that spanned the globe. He had started by renting video equipment from UC San Diego, where he was studying art, to film the Los Angeles riots that led to the killing of Chicano journalist Ruben Salazar. Hoagland was arrested with his equipment during the riots. In 1979, his political leanings took him to Nicaragua to shoot the epic revolution in which the grassroots Sandinista movement overthrew the despotic family dynasty of Anastasio Somoza. He also spent time as a war photographer in Beirut but returned to El Salvador in 1980. His covers for *Newsweek* (the pinnacle for a war photographer) included, on January 16, 1984, victims of the death squads in a gruesome photo. The headline asked, "Can They Be Stopped?" In the last six months of his life, four of his photos had made the cover of *Newsweek*. He received numerous death threats from right-wing groups.

In January 1981, a car in which he was riding in El Salvador ran over a land mine. He and the war photographer Susan Meiselas, perhaps the most celebrated female photographer in El Salvador during the war, were wounded. Their companion, South African journalist Ian Mates, died from the injuries he sustained. Four days later, French photographer Olivier Rebbot, working for *Newsweek*, was shot and killed by a sniper.

For Hoagland, the end came on a road with a Salvadoran army patrol. For years, the last six shots in his camera have been posted on the Internet. They show photos of a patrol of Salvadoran soldiers, then a picture of a soldier turning toward him. The last two photos are of his feet as he falls to the ground, still working to document what was around him. He had been 50 yards ahead of another group of journalists. He was 36.

Torgerson's companion on his last day, Richard Cross, was a similar soul. In fact, David Levi Strauss's book *Between the Eyes* devotes a chapter to the photography of Hoagland and Cross and how it struggled for American attention amid advertising messages that filled the magazines in which their battle photos were published.

Cross had earned a degree in magazine journalism from Northwestern University, worked as a Peace Corps volunteer in Colombia while doing ethnology work, and published his photos in a book about Black farming society in Colombia. In 1979, he went to Nicaragua and, like Hoagland, was deeply influenced by the Sandinista revolution. His work was just as inspired, appearing in major U.S. magazines and picked up around the world. He was nominated by the Associated Press for a Pulitzer for his Nicaraguan photos. One of his most memorable photos, a terrifying portrait of a group of Salvadoran soldiers, appeared in *Paris Match*, *Mother Jones*, and on the cover of *The Economist*.

In *Between the Eyes*, Strauss quoted Cross's academic advisor, Richard Chalfen, who said this about Cross's work: "As a young thinking photojournalist, Richard was not satisfied with merely getting the 'right' picture—an image that conformed to an often unarticulated set of editorial decisions, sometimes aesthetic, sometimes political, as imposed by photo agencies and staffs of popular publications. It became clear that Richard felt a growing sense of responsibility for images he 'took from' people and 'gave to' the viewing public. The political context of image publications became an increasingly important problem in his practice of photography."

In Central America, it was easier for photographers to use their work to tell the deeper truth of the war than it was for print journalists. The latter were bound by the "he said, she said" framing that required even the most evil acts to get framed—which is to say, denied—by a government spokesperson. Typically, these were given the same weight as the reporter's firsthand observation. Just to survive in El Salvador, journalists had to toe a careful line. Their stories were closely monitored not only by the government, but also by the death squads and paramilitary forces. These groups routinely issued death lists of reporters they felt were too sympathetic to the poor or to the FMLN.

Perhaps no incident more chilled journalists in El Salvador than the killing of four Dutch journalists on March 17, 1982: Koos Koster, Jan Kuiper, Hans ter Laag, and Johannes "Joop" Willemsen. The four were among the more than 700 foreign journalists in El Salvador to report on the upcoming elections for the National Assembly. Both the Reagan Administration and the Salvadoran government were working hard to show that, despite the fact that there was a brutal civil war going on and that death squads were operating against any form of government opposition, a "free and fair" election could take place.

Just under a week before, on March 11, the four had been arrested by the Treasury Police and questioned for four hours about their contacts with leftists. In 1980, Koster had produced a TV report that was shown widely in Holland describing how civil defense units organized by the Salvadoran government were also working as death squads. The Salvadoran military viewed the report as sympathetic to the FMLN. On March 7, 1982, Koster and the other Dutch journalists visited the infamous Mariona prison to interview prisoners who were considered FMLN sympathizers. They filmed scars that the prisoners said were the result of torture, and they were thanked by the prisoners for their sympathetic report from 1980.

In 1982, the journalists were staying in the Hotel Alameda. A four-story hotel not far from the Camino Real, it was a haven for international and U.S. reporters on a budget. Koster intended to meet with members of the FMLN outside of San Salvador in guerrilla-controlled territory near Chalatenango. In a preliminary contact with a guerrilla courier, Koster put his Hotel Alameda room number on a slip of paper. The courier was followed by government security members who found the courier's papers as he tried to elude them near the hotel.

A decade later, Treasury Police Director-General Col. Francisco Antonio Moran admitted that he had received the name of Koster and his room number. He ordered Koster brought to Treasury Police headquarters for questioning. There, Koster denied knowing any members of the FMLN. According to documents published by the Truth Commission, as he released the Dutch TV reporter, "Colonel Moran warned Koster to be careful because subversive elements knew that he was in the country."

The next day, photographs of Koster and his three companions appeared in the San Salvador newspaper along with a press release from the armed forces press office. The newspaper article was headlined "Foreign Journalist a Contact for Sub-versives" and indicated that Koster's personal papers had been found on a "terrorist." Fellow journalists warned the four to leave the country, because their lives might be in danger. But they disregarded the warnings and hired a German journalist to act as a driver, paying him $100 to take them into guerrilla -held territory.

On the morning of March 17, the four Dutch and the German driver headed out of San Salvador in a minibus with the words "PRENSA-TV" (PRESS-TV) taped on the windows. They met up with a 15-yearold who was to be their guide and headed out of San Salvador toward Chalatenango late in the afternoon.

Near the El Paraiso military barracks north of San Salvador, they noticed that they were being followed by a Jeep Chero-kee, the vehicle of choice of Salvadoran death squads. Less than a kilometer from their arranged meeting area, the Chero-kee turned off. The journalists met a group of guerrillas near Santa Rita who were to be their guides. The Dutch unloaded their TV equipment, their German driver headed back to San Salvador, and the four set out from the road toward a nearby hill. They had gone about 250 meters when they came under heavy rifle and machine-gun fire.

The leader of the military ambush, Sgt. Mario Canizales Espinoza, later said that although he saw that some of the members of the group were taller than the average Salvador-an, he assumed they were armed and guerrilla fighters. When two of these "tall men" attempted to escape from the ambush, he "came down the hill in pursuit of them and shot and killed them with his M-16 from a distance of about 25 meters." Espinoza and members of the military claimed that the ambush was routine and occurred because the route the journalists had taken was a known "guerrilla supply line."

In the wake of the journalists' deaths, the first reports by the government made similar assertions, indicating that the journalists had been killed in "crossfire" between Salvadoran soldiers and guerrillas. But subsequent investigations and autopsies revealed that the journalists had been ambushed by Salvadoran soldiers who knew they were in the area and apparently had lain in wait for their arrival. Soldiers from the nearby El Paraiso barracks, for example, said that a meeting of higher-ups in the military and members of the U.S.-trained Atonal Rapid Deployment Infantry Battalion took place to plan the ambush of the journalists.

Suspicions about the shooting had grown after the army failed to disclose the deaths for 24 hours. When other journalists arrived at the scene, they found evidence that the Dutch had been stripped of some of their clothes, a classic death-squad move, and their bodies had been dragged around the area of the shooting. In a thinly veiled warning to other journalists, the Defense Ministry said journalists were "endangering themselves" if they continued to meet with guerrillas.

After news of the killings reached San Salvador, the German driver who had originally driven the journalists to the Santa Rita Road area made inquiries about the shooting to the military press office. Later that day, he began to receive threatening phone calls and was told "there was a fifth coffin ready for him."

The Dutch government demanded an inquiry into the shooting, but after a Salvadoran judge opened an official inquiry, she abruptly resigned and asked for asylum outside El Salvador. She said she had received anonymous threats.

On the same day the military had announced the Dutch deaths, a list with 25 names—24 journalists, plus one U.S. embassy official—had been dropped off at a Salvadoran radio station. It was signed by the "Anti-Communist Alliance for El Salvador," and proclaimed that "these are the ones responsible for the international discredit to our armed forces and principal accomplices of Soviet-Cuban-Sandinista communism, which wants to take over our beloved homeland." It also threatened "death to the traitors of democracy." It appeared these 25 would be in grave danger if they stayed in El Salvador.

The list included the four Dutch journalists who had been murdered, as well as the AP's Joe Frazier, John Newhagen, Raymond Bonner, Shirley Christian, Alan Riding, and Harry Mattison; *The Washington Post*'s Karen DeYoung; UPI's Juan Tamayo; and the U.S. Embassy officer Howard Lane. A declassified March 1982 memo from the Embassy to the State Department indicated that they planned extra security for Lane. "The Embassy is taking this list seriously," the memo read. "There are reports today concerning violence perpetrated against several foreign journalists in Northern El Salvador. The threats may be in earnest."

The story that ran about the list in *The Sacramento Bee* followed a kind of war-zone code, writing, about the journalists' deaths and the list, that "there were no indications the two developments were linked. Given what is now known about military and death squad activity, there is no way the two incidents could not be linked."

United Press International, in its un-bylined story March 19, noted that the shootings had occurred just three miles from El Paraiso, where U.S. Green Beret advisors were training Salvadoran soldiers. Residents in the area said there were guerrillas in the region but that there had been no activity in the area for months.

Even classified dispatches from the U.S. Embassy, later obtained by the National Security Archives, hinted that the Dutch had been murdered by the military in an ambush planned by military officers, for their political journalism. On the day the deaths were announced, the State Department issued a public statement: "We deeply regret the deaths of the four Dutch journalists.... We regard it as a tragedy when the press, in pursuit of its own profession, pays such a price." But State Department documents later declassified indicate the U.S. government knew of numerous instances and evidence of the military going after journalists.

The Salvadoran Truth Commission, which later investigated many of the massacres and killings by the military, concluded the four were killed in an ambush "planned in advance by the commander of the Fourth Infantry Brigade, Col. Mario Reyes Mena, with the knowledge of other officers at the El Paraiso barracks ... and was carried out by a patrol of soldiers from the Atonal Battalion." By the time the Truth Commission report came out, the war was over and the perpetrators had faded back into Salvadoran society. Journalists no longer had to hide, but there was not going to be much in the way of accountability, and certainly no accountability for U.S. complicity.

Small Steps Toward Absolution

The Salvadoran Civil War finally ended in 1992, in UN-brokered peace negotiations between the FMLN and Salvadoran government. This also yielded the Truth Commission, which, according to its mandate, "shall have the task of investigating serious acts of violence that have occurred since 1980 and whose impact on society urgently demands that the public should know the truth."

In a more-than-300-page report, the commission concluded that the military had conducted an extensive campaign of violence against its civilian opponents, and that the government knew much more about these seemingly extrajudicial killings than it had let on. For example, the commission's report revealed that the government had known almost immediately who had killed the three American nuns and missionary, but covered it up. The military also knew who was behind the death squads and who had assassinated the popular Archbishop of San Salvador, Oscar Romero, after he delivered a critical sermon condemning military violence against civilians.

The Truth Commission looked into the disappearance of trade union members, students, and peasant leaders, but it also covered violence inflicted by the left. In probably the most detailed accounting of the killing of four U.S. Marines at a San Salvador restaurant in June 1985, the Truth Commission concluded that a faction of the FMLN that claimed responsibility had violated "rules of international humanitarian law."

The four Marines were part of the Embassy guard unit. According to the Truth Commission, they were regulars at Chili's restaurant in the tony Zona Rosa neighborhood of San Salvador and often spent off-duty hours there. They had arrived there around 8:30 p.m. on June 19, 1985. None carried arms, and all were in civilian clothes. A pickup truck pulled up and began firing at the group, killing Marine Sgt. Thomas Handwork, Cpl. Patrick Kwiatkowski, Sgt. Bobby Dickson, and Cpl. Gregory Webber. Nine civilians in Chili's also were killed, including two American businesspeople.

Members of the FMLN later said that their attack on U.S. soldiers was in fact an attack on allies of the Salvadoran military, and justified because these particular soldiers had been identified as working with the Salvadoran military and were involved in "intelligence" work for the U.S. The Truth Commission found no such evidence for the latter assertion and declared that since the four were not combatants, their killing "was a violation of international humanitarian law." Four Salvadorans ultimately were arrested for the attack, though three of them said they confessed after torture.

The Truth Commission report also contained damning evidence about the complicity of U.S. Embassy guards in the disappearance of at least two Salvadorans. Francisco Arnulfo Ventura and Jose Humberto Mejia, law students at the University of El Salvador, were arrested January 22, 1980, in the parking lot of the U.S. Embassy following a demonstration that was broken up by the military.

The U.S. Embassy parking lot was one of the most heavily defended areas near the embassy and, according to the Truth Commission, Ventura and Mejia had gone there after the military opened fire on a demonstration in downtown San Salvador. They were at the Embassy gate when members of the Salvadoran National Guard arrested them and took them into the parking lot, which was patrolled by U.S. soldiers. Shortly afterward, a private car entered the parking lot and the two men were put in the car trunk and driven off. They were never seen again.

U.S. Embassy officials said they knew about the students' arrest but that U.S. Marines did not participate. They also said that the members of the Salvadoran National Guard who had been guarding the Embassy had brought the students into the [Embassy] courtyard to search them and had kept them there. They added that shortly afterward, the two young men had been taken out of the Embassy.

Gen. Carlos Eugenio Vides Casanova, head of the National Guard and one of the most powerful military leaders in El Salvador, denied the U.S. Embassy reports, in effect denying there had been any arrest. The man who was most linked to death squads in El Salvador blew off the government of the United States and indicated that no Salvadoran was safe even on the grounds of the U.S. Embassy guarded by U.S. Marines.

Members of the two students' families looked in traditional dumping grounds for death-squad victims, but their remains were never found.

Three months later, the Truth Commission reported, "The death squad known as 'Ejército Secreto Anti-Comunista' published a list of names which included people who had already been murdered or disappeared. The names of Francisco Arnulfo Ventura and Jose Humberto Mejia were on the list. At the end of the list was an exhortation which read '… help us get rid of all these traitors and criminal communists. The country will thank you for it.'"

If "disappearing" student demonstrators, killing American nuns, and assassinating archbishops were all fair game for the security forces and their death squads, there was a particular hatred saved for members of the media, both local and international. Top military officials on many occasions claimed the international press was sympathetic to the guerrillas and aided their propaganda campaign. Outside the public eye, the military took action to retaliate. The rules of engagement were to shoot first, not ask any questions, and later blame the deaths on the guerrillas.

Perhaps the most disturbing finding of the Truth Commission was its confirmation that members of the U.S.-trained Atlácatl Battalion, the Salvadoran military's elite combat unit, "deliberately and systematically killed a group of more than 200 men, women, and children, constituting the entire civilian population" of El Mozote on December 11, 1981. The commission concluded that 85 percent of the victims were children.

The massacre was part of a major offensive in the department of Morazán, long a guerrilla stronghold, or, as it was known in the Salvadoran military parlance, a "red zone." The offensive was led by U.S.-trained Lt. Col. Jose Domingo Monterrosa Barrios. A specific aim was to capture the guerrillas' clandestine radio station, Radio Venceremos. Another was to "dry up the sea" of peasants who nominally supported the guerrillas.

A detailed and horrifying account of what happened next is contained in Mark Danner's *The Massacre at El Mozote*. The villagers of Mozote were forced out of their homes, with the men being led to a nearby church and the women crammed into a residence. Young women and female children were taken into the hills, where they were raped and murdered. The men were decapitated or, when that took too much time, taken into the nearby brush and shot. Women were also led into the nearby hills and shot. The best estimates are that almost 700 innocent civilians were slaughtered.

The story was first reported by *The New York Times'* Raymond Bonner and the war photographer Susan Meiselas. Alma Guillermoprieto, of *The Washington Post*, arrived a day later and told Danner she could smell burned bodies some distance from Mozote. She found the church filled with charred bodies. Both Bonner and Guillermoprieto were able to interview the lone survivor of the attack, a village woman named Rufina Amaya. She had escaped while they were leading women into the brush, and she hid there all night.

Meiselas later wrote about the experience of walking through Mozote when it was filled with dead bodies: "The big lesson for me was that I saw and photographed what seemed like evidence but there was no way for me to confirm or prove the number of dead. Nearly a thousand villagers had been killed but we mostly came across burned fragments. Possession of the evidence can be endangering…. There had been a certainty about going to Mozote. We didn't focus on the risk. We felt we had to do it. We had to know what had happened."

When the *Times* and *Post* published front-page stories of a possible Salvadoran military massacre, it threw the newly inaugurated Reagan Administration into a frenzy. Congress, concerned about the war, wanted the administration on a regular basis to certify that Salvador was complying with human rights protocols. A massacre of innocent civilians, including what may have been more than 100 children, was, to put it mildly, a problem. The Reagan Administration went so far as to put pressure on *The New York Times* to withdraw their reporter from El Salvador after he filed reports on the killing. Echoing the Reagan Administration, *The Wall Street Journal* ran an editorial blasting Bonner's credibility and argued that no massacre had taken place. Faced with a torrent of right-wing criticism of Bonner, inside and outside the U.S. and Salvador governments, *New York Times* Executive Editor A. M. Rosenthal ordered Bonner out of El Salvador and back to New York for "training."

The Embassy had sent Todd Greentree and embassy military attaché Major John McKay to investigate. Greentree had come to see me in the hospital after I was shot, and I still have the business card he gave me then. On its foldout, he had scrawled "George, Good Luck." He went on to have a distinguished career in the foreign service, serving in Afghanistan, writing a book on counterinsurgency warfare, and making many public appearances as a lecturer. I have followed that career and felt grateful for his kindness to me when I was hurt. But, learning more about the complicity of the U.S. in the worst brutalities of the Salvadoran Civil War, I have also discovered a troubling fact: Greentree helped with the cover-up of the massacre at Mozote.

The Salvadoran military would not provide Greentree and McKay with an escort into El Mozote, so Greentree interviewed soldiers and officers in the Morazán province. His conclusion, contained in a cable over the name of Ambassador Deane Hinton, was that there had been a firefight. But the cable only relied on military accounts, which all denied a massacre.

Major McKay later told writer Mark Danner, "In the end, we went up there and we didn't want to find that anything horrible had happened."

Greentree later admitted to Mark Danner that the cable was not a "satisfactory account." What's more, it came the day before the Reagan Administration certified El Salvador as comporting with human rights standards—an obvious falsehood. The Greentree report helped the Reagan Administration justify the war, which would go on for another decade and ultimately take 75,000 Salvadoran lives. It was just one of several massacres and wanton killings by the military, from the murders at Río Lempa to the killing of seven Jesuit priests in San Salvador. In a detailed 2023 examination of Salvadoran military actions, *El Salvador: Volume 1: Crisis, Coup and Uprising 1970–1983*, David François reported that around the same time as Mozote, military massacres occurred in La Ranchería, Los Toriles, La Joya, Poza Honda, El Rincón, El Potrero, Yancolo, Flor de Muerto, and Cerro Pando.

Greentree's own book describes Mozote as the "largest single atrocity to occur during the civil war or anywhere in Latin America in the second half of the 20th Century." He even footnotes the number of victims: 767 noncombatant men, women, and children. There is no mention of his role in failing to reveal the true nature of what had occurred. Greentree was a junior foreign service officer at the time, and it seems he was not about to take on Ronald Reagan.

In late 1992, as the war was winding down, the Tutela Legal, the Salvadoran human rights office, requested that a team of Argentinian forensic anthropologists, led by internationally known Mercedes Doretti, exhume the mass grave sites at Mozote to determine the cause of death of so many innocent civilians. In the first burial site unearthed, the team found the skeletons of 117 individuals, including a pregnant woman and many children. Shell casings were found in the burial site and the adjoining area. Doretti was able to conclude that the casings carried the telltale marking of their origin, the Lake City Army Ammunition Plant. The plant manufactured 1.4 billion rounds of ammunition each year for the U.S. Army and other governments. The bullets that killed the villagers in Mozote had been supplied to the Salvadoran military, which used them to conduct massacres and killings. (Today the Lake City plant continues to churn out ammunition, though the property it is on is now considered by the EPA as a Superfund site, contaminated by years of dumping toxic chemicals into burn pits and onto the ground.)

In 2023, I asked Greentree about the impact of the cable he had helped craft to Washington in the wake of the massacre. He responded, "You can rely on Mark Danner's book with confidence. Congress could have gone further in demanding an investigation into El Mozote. My report, as compromised in editing as it was, combined with the *New York Times* and *Washington Post* reports, was more than sufficient evidence.

The problem was not so much the fog of war as it was Democrats' reluctance to block RR [President Reagan] from certifying, because they had no desire of being accused of 'losing' El Salvador following Jimmy Carter's failure in Nicaragua."

Raymond Bonner later said that in his interview of Greentree for a documentary on Mozote, Greentree said, "The United States was complicit." He told Bonner that the massacre was carried out by the Atlácatl Battalion, which had just returned from training in the U.S. at the School of the Americas at Ft. Benning. It was the battalion's first combat after their training.

I thanked Greentree for his comfort and aid when I had been shot. My feelings toward his role were mixed. Maybe he could have slowed the war with a more accurate report of the massacre. Maybe he was up against Republicans and Democrats who wanted to beat communism, at whatever cost. But how could you not be moved and enraged by the deaths of so many innocents, including so many children?

Perhaps the most disquieting part of Mark Danner's book is the appendix, in which he lists the names, ages, and occupations of those who were slaughtered at El Mozote, as well as in the communities of La Joya, Los Toriles, Jocote Amarillo, Cerro Pando, and Joateca.

The Truth Commission, for its part, concluded that higher-ups in the Salvadoran military knew about the massacre at Mozote and deliberately covered it up. What is missing throughout the Truth Commission report, however heroic its work and findings, is a crucial piece of the puzzle of what went wrong in El Salvador during the dirty war of 1980–1992: the role of the United States and its obsession with fighting armed peasants who just wanted a decent life but were condemned as "communists." There is no description of the role of the United States and its military advisors and intelligence officers in El Salvador during this period. No mention of the role of the U.S. in training soldiers that participated in some of the most brutal massacres.

For many years, the U.S. gave shelter to some of the most brutal Salvadoran leaders. In 1989, the U.S. government granted visas to Gen. Jose Guillermo Garcia, the defense minister and commander of all security forces, and Gen. Carlos Eugenio Vides Casanova, head of the National Guard and later the defense minister, when they retired. The U.S. government had agreed to provide them sanctuary after they claimed they and their families had been threatened in El Salvador. President Ronald Reagan awarded Casanova the Legion of Merit, one of the highest awards a foreign military officer can received from the U.S. government. After the signing of the peace accords, both Garcia and Casanova took up a comfortable life in Florida, far from the chaos of El Salvador.

But soon after their arrival, the U.S. Congress passed the 1991 Torture Victim Protection Act, which allowed civil suits to be brought against government and military officials who engaged in systematic torture in foreign countries. It was partly aimed at giving U.S. citizens a chance to sue torturers in Iraq and Iran, but its first case involved torture in Guatemala.

In 2000, a Florida jury acquitted Casanova and Garcia of civil charges in the 1980 killing of the American churchwomen, even though the Truth Commission concluded that Casanova, head of the National Guard, must have been aware of who carried out the killings. The case was denied on appeal, and in 2003, the U.S. Supreme Court refused to hear the case.

In 2002, Garcia and Casanova were hit with a $55 million federal jury verdict, upheld by a federal appeals court, after three Salvadorans sued them and accused them of torture. Press accounts indicated Casanova was forced to hand over $300,000 to the torture victims.

One of those plaintiffs was Dr. Juan Romagoza Arce, who was practicing as a surgeon in Chalatenango, one of the most contested regions of El Salvador. In December 1980, while Arce was conducting a mass health clinic, a National Guard truck pulled up and its officers began firing into the crowd. Arce was taken to the El Paraiso (Paradise) garrison and re-called in federal court how he had been hung upside down by chains, prodded with electric shocks, and sexually assaulted. In his testimony, he recalled how Casanova had visited him in his cell. After the visit, the torture worsened. When he was finally released, he had lost 50 pounds and weighed 70 pounds. He fled El Salvador, spent time in Mexico, and finally ended up in San Francisco, where he worked as a janitor. He finally was able use his medical training to volunteer at a San Francisco clinic whose patients were mostly from Latin America. But he was never able to practice surgery because his fingers were severely damaged after being wrapped in metal wire by his torturers.

Another victim, Neris Gonzalez, a church worker at the time of her detention, said she suffered 12 days of torture and rape at the hands of National Guard troops. At the time, she was eight months pregnant, and after her release, her baby died as a result of its injuries. After the verdict, she told *The New York Times*, "The Salvadoran military bears responsibility for what we, as a people, suffered."

In 2011, both Casanova and Garcia faced deportation in what *The New York Times* reported as a lawsuit brought by the Department of Homeland Security and hailed "by human rights advocates as the first time a special human rights office at the DHS has brought immigration charges against a top-ranking foreign military commander."

Both ultimately lost their cases and were deported. A judge in the Garcia deportation case said he was involved in a number of human rights violations, and press accounts noted the judge, Michael C. Horn of the Immigration Court in Miami, said Garcia "played a direct role in some of the most egregious killings and torture in El Salvador at a time when Washington was supporting the Salvadoran military in its battle against leftist insurgents." His ruling states there was "clear and convincing evidence" that Garcia participated in at least 11 major human rights violations, including the assassination of Archbishop Oscar Romero."

On April 8, 2015, U.S. immigration officials deported Casanova. On January 8, 2016, immigration officials deported Garcia.

In further evidence that some of the worst perpetrators of torture and terror killings could be brought to justice, General Garcia and Treasury Police Director-General Francisco Antonio Moran were ordered arrested on October 13, 2022, by a Salvadoran judge. They were charged with the murder of the four Dutch journalists on March 17, 1982. The judge also ordered the arrest of the commander of the Army Fourth

Infantry Brigade and the former chief of the Army's Joint General Staff.

El Salvador had convened a Truth Commission to reveal the deep and violent role of the military and its death squads. It named names and, in cases like Garcia and Moran's, helped lead to court trials.

The U.S., on the other hand, shrugged: Sure, it kicked two evil men out of their comfortable Florida lifestyles, but it never reckoned with its own complicity, and it never made reparations to the Salvadoran people. As the years went on, it seemed more and more urgent that, in some small way, I try to.

My Search Begins

As the twentieth century closed, it seemed a time of new beginnings and stout resolutions. I had put off confronting Gilberto's death for a long time. When I decided to begin my search for Gilberto in 2000, I assumed I would eventually find his family, leave flowers at his grave, and neatly put a bow on a painful but interesting part of my life. I would, I thought, succeed where my own country had failed. It was the turn of the century and a time for new beginnings.

Like most fairy-tale scenarios, it did not come true.

In 2001, I visited the main cemetery in San Salvador, where they still keep huge ledgers of every burial dating back decades. Several cemetery workers kindly steered me to the room where the ledgers were kept, and a clerk pulled down the ledgers for 1981. I had seen enough television that I figured this was the moment. The name Gilberto Moran would be there, maybe a few weeks out of place, and then the burial workers would guide me to his grave.

There were numerous listings for 1981. It was a busy time for the main cemetery in San Salvador. In that section of the cemetery, there were plenty of graves for those in their teens and twenties. But none of them was inscribed *Gilberto Moran.*

I scoured the Internet and tracked down other journalists who had been working in El Salvador at the same time. No one seemed to remember Moran. Nor did they know Steve Patten, who had been with us when we were shot. He, like Moran, seemed to have vanished.

Yet I kept turning up enough clues to think I should keep going.

In the November/December 1981 issue of the bulletin of the North American Congress on Latin America (NACLA), for example, a well-informed writer with the byline Rufus Jones described Gilberto's death and was sharply critical of mainstream American journalists. I had long ago filed the piece away, wondering if Larry Bullard, a member of Steve Patten's film crew, might have written it using an alias to protect himself.

The article opens by noting that if TV were your main source of news, you would have never heard of Gilberto Moran. The reporter was at the scene of the Soyapango shooting with other journalists. After days of trying to get footage of refugee camps, corrupt Salvadoran Army officers, and evidence of a military massacre of civilians on the air in the U.S., Jones wrote that his colleagues were in a heightened journalistic mode because they "finally [had] a U.S. victim"—me.

"There is an air of excitement inside the bureau which gradually turns to disappointment," Jones wrote. "We had made the mistake of filming the war instead of the wounded American. In the words of [our] chief: It was good try but you missed the nut."

"Having missed the nut, we are immediately sent back to get an interview with George Thurlow. However, he is still recovering from surgery and cannot be disturbed," Jones added.

In the end, despite the fact they had interviewed Joaquin Zuniga about the involvement of the Treasury Police, the edited piece that appeared that night on national television never mentioned Zuniga or Moran. "It was mainly about the wounding of George Thurlow," Jones wrote.

Jones's story did contain an intriguing postscript. It detailed how, after Gilberto Moran's death, his family had fled to Honduras. "They were followed there by Salvadoran police who searched their house and accused Gilberto of having worked for the popular forces. The family was subjected to this harassment despite the personal condolences they had received from President Duarte on the death of their son at the hands of the guerrillas.

"Gilberto's wife and daughter are now in the United States and are applying for political asylum."

But from there, the trail has grown cold. I have talked to dozens, if not hundreds, of Salvadorans about war records and none has a good lead. Local papers contain no accounts of Gilberto's death, other than one story that appeared the next day in *El Diario de Hoy*. As for Gilberto's wife, I contacted a very high-level State Department official who candidly said there was no chance I would be able to track her down with U.S. government documents. The documents were endless, and privacy laws would bar their release to a third-party journalist.

On one trip to El Salvador, I was driving through the city when I spotted a medical specialist with the last name Moran. I told the cab driver to turn around, and I walked into the office. After I told my story to a seemingly skeptical receptionist, the doctor finally came out. No, he knew nothing of a Gilberto Moran. He noted that there were many Morans in El Salvador. Ironically, two of the most evil men in El Salvador, both linked to organizing and directing death squads, are also Morans: Treasury Police Director-General Col. Francisco Antonio Moran and National Guard intelligence director Mario Denis Moran.

We are now approaching the 43rd anniversary of Gilberto Moran's death, and I am no closer to making restitution to his family. The search has become the story.

She Has the Photo and the Pain

A little less than a year after my time in El Salvador, I was thumbing through an issue of *In These Times*, a progressive publication that covered stories most reporters couldn't get past their editors. I spotted an article on El Salvador and, as I often did, glanced at it quickly, tore it out, and tossed it in a pile of clippings and articles.

Many years later, as I was culling all the dead-end articles about topics I never would have time to investigate or illuminate, I picked up the *In These Times* article and looked more closely.

It was one of those haunted moments in life.

The picture was dark. It showed a group of people huddled around a body in a road. A trio of nonchalant soldiers stand by. I think it was the shirt that snagged my subconscious.

On the day of the shooting, Gilberto Moran had been wearing a baseball-style shirt, with green sleeves and a white torso. As I looked at the body in the photo, then at the man standing next to it, I realized that it was a photo taken of Gilberto Moran lying dead and Steve Patten standing over him. Patten is looking in the plastic bag we had put all our belongings into: our tape recorders, water bottles, extra film, and note pads.

Stunned by the photo, I put it away. Over the years, I would pull it out, never show it to anybody, put it back away. I would ponder how it was that this instant in time had been captured by a photographer, and then lost in my files.

Until 2002.

By then, I had begun my search for Moran's family, and I wanted to find out everything I could about what happened after the ambulance whisked me away to the Policlínica. So I pulled the photo back out. The credit line read: "1981 Diane Schmidt." Surely, I thought, the photographer who had shown up immediately after the shooting and shot photos of the event could be a gold mine of information. Maybe she could tell me what had been going on, why we had stumbled into a death

Steve Patten, right, stands over the body of Gilberto Moran just minutes after the shooting. Photo by Diane Joy Schmidt.

trap, what the Treasury Police had said in the aftermath of the shooting, even where Gilberto's body had been taken.

I had written for *In These Times* a few times myself, so I had some sense of how they worked, and expected they would not be able to help me find Schmidt some 20 years after she'd sold them the photo. But maybe, with the revolution of the Internet, I could find her myself.

I put Diane Schmidt's name into Google and hit return. As everybody who has conducted a blind search knows, common names like this can lead you to everything from masters' dissertations to 5K race results, but on page 66, one detail looked like it might be promising: A Diane Schmidt was cited in the University of Chicago admissions office website as the photographer who provided artistic shots of the campus architecture.

I emailed the University of Chicago office of admissions, and they sent me a phone number of a photographer named Diane Schmidt who lived in Albuquerque. I called and left a message on the answering machine asking if this Diane Schmidt had ever been in El Salvador and if she had sold a photo of a road-side shooting to *In These Times*. I gave her an email address to respond.

She took a while to respond, and she seemed cautious: Yes, she had been in El Salvador. But who was I and what did I want?

I mailed her the articles I had written about El Salvador in the '80s, and in response, she said she had sold *In These Times* the photo of Gilberto but had no unique memory of it. She had shot a lot of photos, she wrote, and a lot of them had been disturbing. I asked her if we could meet in person, in Albuquerque.

Soldiers haul Gilberto Moran's body into the back of an army truck. Photo by Diane Joy Schmidt.

At first, she said that these were old stories, chapters of her life that she had closed. Finally, she agreed to meet for breakfast in the summer of 2002, at the Indigo Crow, a small restaurant in the Corrales neighborhood of Albuquerque.

Diane told me that when she had returned from El Salvador in 1981, as a 22-year-old photographer, she had bound up all her negatives, stuck them in a box, and never opened them again—not until I had called her, out of the blue, asking about one of her photographs. Now, she brought out a folder containing the photos she had taken during her stay in El Salvador. These didn't include any photos of Gilberto Moran, so I asked her if she could look for the roll taken on April 29, 1981, and send me a proof sheet. She agreed, but she emphasized that she wanted all our conversations to stay off the record. These conversations "brought back many painful feelings," she wrote in an email, and she wanted to tell her own story when she was ready. When she sent me a proof sheet of the photos of Gilberto Moran, she sent it in a format that would ensure I could never reproduce them.

Her story was disturbing. She had traveled to El Salvador much like I did, with idealism and a dream to be a journalist. She left there disenchanted, bitter, and very fearful. Photos she had taken, including many of death and destruction, were controversial. I will honor her wish not to share more of her experiences—that is for her to do, and she has written both a screenplay and a book manuscript about her experiences. The book, which she says is currently titled *Darkening of the Light*, may be self-published. It would join a very small collection of memoirs by journalists and authors. Like many of the Salvadorans I have met over the years, I think most journalists want to put this part of their career in a box that is stored at the bottom of a closet. And of course, there are no big advances or retainers for books about the El Salvadoran tragedy, even though, in the years since El Salvador, Diane has won numerous awards for both her writing and photography.

But I can share that, in an early draft Diane sent of her story, she wrote of photographing 17-year-old Adalberto Martinez after he had been shot in the back of the head by Treasury Police a few blocks from their headquarters in Ciudad Delgado. She watched as the boy's mother came running up, wailing. It was just two weeks before my shooting.

On April 29, Diane had been hanging out with the ABC TV crew and had heard the urgent report of journalists being shot in Soyapango. She had rushed out with the other journalists, and she took a dozen photos of Gilberto Moran. Lying by the road. Soldiers looking at the body. Three soldiers picking him up by arms and legs and hauling him into the back of an army truck. His body lying in the back of the truck.

No different than hundreds and even thousands of similar shots of the Salvadoran dead being hauled off into the afternoon and night and day.

When I look at them over and over again, it's like it was yesterday.

As this book was ready to go to a printer, Diane Schmidt agreed to sell me the Moran photos. We had been in conversation about their use for almost 20 years.

Diane was not able to tell me what happened to Gilberto's body. But being able to see her photographs made my own experience—and the urgency of trying to do something about it—hit more viscerally. She didn't know where his body was, let alone his family, but I would keep looking for someone else who could.

Back at the Camino Real

In 2005, I went back to the Camino Real in San Salvador. At the door—as he had been for most of the past 21 years—was Tomas Flores, then 49 years old. He was diminutive, bespectacled, and, I learned, had been a waiter at the Camino Real when I was there in 1981. Maybe, I thought, he could help me find Gilberto Moran.

He could not, but at the coffee shop across the street—smart, and crisply dressed out of uniform—he had other stories to tell me.

During the war, Flores recalled, there were only journalists, stringers, and hangers-on living in the Camino Real—some 250 of them. They were all on the second floor. More than 100 Salvadorans worked at the hotel as drivers, translators, camera people, and couriers. At the time, the banquet rooms were all closed. There were no fancy receptions or big business conferences. Only the journalists on limited expense accounts. Flores remembered the bomb that had knocked out many of the hotel windows just before I'd arrived. "Three guerrillas triggered the bomb," he said. A big truck with soldiers then began to fire at them, and "some of the bullets hit the hotel."

He also recalled the police coming to the hotel to search the offices of journalists there who were suspected of communicating with the guerrillas. "They destroyed everything in one room," said Flores. They confiscated two of the police radios the journalists used to monitor army and security forces actions. It was a dangerous time. In 1981, there was a 7 p.m. curfew, and "every night, the journalists would go to the bar. They were talking about the news of the war. They drank to lose their fear." (They also used marijuana and cocaine.) "When you left the hotel and went into the streets, maybe you didn't come back," Flores recalled.

Flores worked six days a week and made $300 a month at the hotel, giving him a comfortable salary and a job with some prestige. He had lived his entire life in Soyapango, the neighborhood where I was shot. He and his wife have a daughter, of whom they are very proud; when we spoke, she was in medical school. During the war, however, his family experienced the fighting that tore through their neighborhood.

During the Final Offensive of January 1981, he and his neighbors could not leave their houses when the guerrillas overran Soyapango. It was a Friday night, and normally Salvadorans buy food on the weekend. But on this weekend, they went without. "All night long, I heard people walking down our street. We did not know what was happening. In the morning, there were many, many guerrillas, hundreds and hundreds, wearing black uniforms."

The guerrillas had planned the Final Offensive to preempt any military moves the incoming Reagan Administration had planned when it took office in late January. But the revolt fizzled when the working-class residents of neighborhoods like Soyapango refused to join the guerrillas and rise up against the army. Not that it protected them from the wrath of the military: They went on, Flores recalled, to drop bombs on Soyapango in retaliation of the guerrilla presence. "Many factories and houses were destroyed."

When the offensive stalled, the guerrillas retreated back into the mountains. But they continued to come back to Soyapango. The guerrillas often burned the buses in the community, meaning workers had no way to get to work. Flores recalled the many attacks on the power station in Agua Caliente, where we were shot. At one point, the bridge over the Agua Caliente River was destroyed. "They attacked the power plant almost every day," Flores recalled.

When Steve, Gilberto, and I walked down that road in 1981 in Soyapango, we were entering an area that had been the scene of fighting for weeks, had suffered military massacres, and was a hostile place for any trio of young men walking down a jungle road.

The next day after speaking with Flores, I went to meet the photographer Arturo Romero. All over the world, anybody who has worked in San Salvador knows him by his nickname: La Muñeca. He has worked for almost 30 years as a photographer in El Salvador, first for the local newspaper *Diario Latino* and, since November 1981, for the AP. His office used to be in Room 201 of the Camino Real.

Now, Romero was working out of the Associated Press offices in Santa Tecla, about nine miles west of downtown San Salvador. When I saw him, it was a slow day and, as at newspaper offices the world over, the place was strewn with newspapers, magazines, and piles of press credentials from every possible event. On the TV was a Mexican show with dancing girls, and on the walls were truck-stop calendars with pretty women in bathing suits.

When I asked Romero about the shooting, he recalled it instantly, but he had no memory of me or my role in it. What he remembered was that Joaquin Zuniga, who had worked for the AP—and here Romero pointed to his own leg—had been badly wounded in the shooting. Romero also remembered Ivan Montecinos, the UPI photographer who shot photos of Zuniga being loaded into an ambulance.

At the AP, Romero recalled, Joe Frazier was the bureau chief to Annie Cabrera and Eloy Aguilar. As for UPI bureau chief John Newhagen, Romero had one word: "loco." He put his finger to his head and moved it in a small circle.

Romero's most vivid memories from the war were of Soyapango and surrounding communities, which made up a kind of belt of misery. Many of the residents of Soyapango were guerrilla sympathizers, Romero said. The Treasury Police had a cuartel there that was constantly being attacked, as was the power plant.

"Every morning, we would go through Soyapango," Romero recalled. "We would go very early in the morning and look for the dead in the streets. I would go with Italian cameraman Marcelo Sandini, John Hoagland, and Ivan Montecinos.

"We were looking for the bodies of the death squads. We would find the white hand on the doors." The notorious death squad Mano Blanco, or White Hand, would paint its moniker on doorways of homes where it had kidnapped or killed suspected guerrilla sympathizers. "First, on our rounds, we would go to Soyapango," he said. "Then we would go to Cuscatancingo and then on to Mariona. Our last stop would be Playón, at the back of the volcano. The birds would be eating the bodies there."

I asked Romero if he had photos from those days that might be helpful. "The AP office burned in 1992 and I lost all my files," he said wistfully. "It was very sad. Twelve years of work."

All I thought of was another dead end. Yet Romero gave me another set of eyes on the dangers of Soyapango and its history as a dumping ground for civilian bodies. He also understood the irony that I could come so very close to finding another chapter, only to discover it had burned in a fire. Of course, I told myself, the search was part of the point, but I thought the search would be easier.

A Daily Diary of Death

It was hard to fathom the amount of suffering that had gone on during the 12 years of civil war, but I wanted to try. Scrapbooks at the Jesuit University of Central America helped.

The UCA is a tree-filled oasis in the northwestern part of San Salvador. While the public University of San Salvador was sacked, looted, and shelled repeatedly during the war, the UCA was largely spared until November 16, 1989. That was when six Jesuit priests, their housekeeper, and her 16-year-old daughter were murdered by the death squads in an apparent attempt at intimidation of church leaders who were sympathetic to the plight of the poor and disenfranchised. (The Truth

Commission would later hold military officials responsible for the conspiracy and the killings.)

When I visited UCA in 2001, I was directed to a collection of seven scrapbooks, filled with clippings from the war, in the library's special collections. Staff allowed me to spend an entire day transcribing the articles. Nobody knows who created the scrapbooks. The articles, all from local newspapers, focus totally on the war and its victims, a daily diary of death.

Two years later, when I returned, the library no longer allowed visitors to turn the pages of the scrapbooks. The docent put gloves on to show them to me and I was not allowed to touch the pages myself. Perhaps they were becoming more precious artifacts with the passing of time, or perhaps the library was under stricter management. In any case, seeing them on both trips drove home how little I knew of what was going on in the country when I arrived.

Some of the contents were familiar, including stories about John J. Sullivan's December 1980 disappearance; the January 1981 land mine that killed Ian Mates and injured Susan Meiselas and John Hoagland; and the January 1981 killing of Olivier Rebbot by a government sniper.

But much was new, and the scale of the violence was staggering. A short article from early 1981 noted that the evangelical pastor Antonio Lopez had been kidnapped two days prior to Sullivan. And on January 12, 1981, the day after Sullivan's disappearance had been formally announced, the government required a curfew from 7 p.m. to 5 a.m. "until calm is restored," with the ominous warning from one official that "Nobody can move about the capital without exposing themselves to losing their life."

Two days later, half a page of the paper was devoted to pictures of the 12 people whose bodies had been found dead near Santa Ana, including the beautiful face of one Maria Aracely Figueroa, age 34.

On January 16, 1981, the paper included articles about both the killing of the journalist Olivier Rebbot and an assertion, from the Salvadoran military press office, that the Commission on Human Rights in El Salvador "was in common cause with the enemies of the country." It was yet another example of how, even as the U.S. government praised the human rights situation in El Salvador, the military was openly hostile and threatening to human rights groups.

Three weeks before I was to arrive in El Salvador, the pace of the bloodshed was picking up. On April 8, 1981, *La Prensa Gráfica* ran a photo of seven bodies lying in a street, one clad only in underwear, from the Treasury Police's massacre in Soyapango. The caption reads: "15-20 terrorists are killed in a confrontation in colonia Montecarmelo in Soyapango, according to the Treasury Police." The Treasury Police, known as the Policía de Hacienda, said that "a fight broke out in two houses and 13 weapons had been captured."

April 9, 1981: Individual photos, like those from a high-school yearbook, of those shot in Soyapango were run. They include one young woman who is not identified; a taxi driver, Mario Mejia Hernandez; Milton Nelson Medina Iglesias; and a photo-lab technician, David Antonio Rosales Monico, 20.

April 25, 1981: A photo of the wealthy businessman Ricardo Sol Meza appeared, along with the news that he was to go before a panel investigating the shootings, at the restaurant in the Sheraton Hotel, of Americans Michael Hammer and Mark Pearlman, who worked for the American Institute for Free Labor Development to promote labor rights in El Salvador. The day before, testimony from the Sheraton employee Sofia Alas de Ramirez implicated the owner of the Sheraton, Hans Crist.

The paper also included, on its front page, a photo of damage from a bomb that went off in Plaza Allegre, destroying an outdoor café; the news that three young men, ages 15, 17, and 21, were kidnapped in San Miguel; and the news that five bodies—four young men and one "stout" woman—had been found throughout the Apopa area.

I arrived at the airport the next day.

April 27, 1981: There were two photos of sisters Melba Yanira and Marlene Cecibel, 16 and 17, who had disappeared in San Salvador the week before.

A headline in one newspaper asserts that "Guerrillas Use Money from U.S. Churches." It goes on to say a document "believed to be captured by the government of El Salvador indicates that money donated by U.S. religious groups for the poor in this country instead has been used by the guerrillas." The paper cites the Reagan Administration as the source of some of the documents. Among the groups cited as conduits for guerrilla money are Oxfam, the World Council of Churches, and Catholic Assistance Services.

This appeared as I was trying to track down Sister Rosa Lillia to give her the $1,000 check from San Francisco religious groups.

A bomb went off two days earlier in front of the Banco de Comercio in San Salvador.

Three days earlier, a 39-year-old vegetable vendor was hacked to death with a machete inside the Central Market in San Salvador.

An 18-year-old was found beaten to death on the road to Sonsonate.

A 20-year-old's body was unearthed in San Salvador.

A 30-year-old woman was shot to death in Colonia Lobato in the capital.

In Cuscatancingo, "subversives" attacked the municipal garrison but were repelled by units of the National Guard.

In Santa Ana, "extremists" attacked the Brigade garrison at 10 p.m. The battle went on for more than an hour. Two people were shot dead in a car that weekend. A "well-dressed youth" was found shot dead.

In Quezaltepeque, an officer in the coffee association was shot dead.

A 58-year-old Salvadoran journalist and photographer, Amadeo Mendizabal Martinez, was shot to death as he was leaving the cathedral in San Miguel. At various times, the paper says, he was president of the Association of Eastern Journalists (AOPI) and a correspondent of *El Diario de Hoy*.

He wrote about the economic problems of eastern El Salvador. His family said he received death threats at various times and was not living at his house: He had moved to San Salvador. He believed the threat had passed, so he returned to *tierra natal*, his birthplace, where "he died riddled with bullets."

On April 28, 1981, my second day in El Salvador, the newspapers noted that a 34-year-old Army captain, Ramon Zelaya, had been killed in Sonsonate with a shot to the stomach.

The same day, the paper reported that guerrillas attacked a command post in La Palma, a place known for its artisan crafts of birds and flowers; that a body was found in the Chiplapa neighborhood of San Salvador; that a bomb burned six autos in the Cene Uraya parking garage; and that there were reports of 10,000 refugees in the city of Berlín, Usulután, because of fighting in the countryside. Also in Usulután, Gloria Orodonez Rodriguez was kidnapped and her body found later.

On the ad pages of the newspaper, there is a large announcement from Vice President Jaime Abdul Gutierrez proclaiming: "People of Salvador are in favor of democracy and peace and against the lies and violence of the terrorists. We are not going to permit foreign interference. The communists are attempting to deceive world opinion."

There is also an official report of the press conference that I attended in the capital at the Army headquarters. Defense Minister Gen. Jose Guillermo Garcia, accompanied by Col. Francisco Adolfo Castillo, Deputy Minister of Defense; Col. Rafael Flores Lima, chief of the Estado Mejor; Col. Jose Edmundo Palacios, head of the First Infantry Brigade; Gen. Carlos Eugenio Vides Casanova, director of the National

Guard; and Lt. Col. Roland Rigoberto Ramos, head of training for the Armed Forces, all were in attendance. The men are quoted suggesting that tranquility reigns in the country. There are people who are involved in terrorism, banditry, pillage, and destruction, Garcia asserts. It is hard to fight against this, and it is not just in El Salvador that the fight is waged, he argues. The bandits attack coffee plantations and cinemas. "What type of help is that to the Salvadoran people?" he argues. Yet the official line is one of coming victory: Lima explains that the situation is in favor of the Armed Forces. He said the armed forces are in total control of the country even as it defends the Constitution.

Elsewhere in the paper, there is a report on the disappearance of the Maryknoll priest Roy Bourgeois; a story about a five-hour battle involving 500 insurgents in Santa Clara, San Vicente; a story about Mexico and Venezuela offering to assist in peace talks in El Salvador; a story about more than 100 refugees fleeing into San Salvador from rural Tecoluca; an account of the testimony from Sol Meza about the killing of two U.S. labor advisors and two Salvadoran labor leaders in the Sheraton Hotel; and a story about a car bomb going off at the building housing the Salvadoran Chamber of Commerce. It was the second time the building had been bombed.

On April 29, 1981, the day I was shot, the newspaper clippings reported more bloodshed and more horror.

In Apopa, seven miles from San Salvador, there was an hour-and-a-half-long attack on a civil defense post.

In Coatepeque, three civil patrol members were killed in action.

Masked men killed three teens and a 20-year-old in Nejapa. The four were agriculture workers. They were taken away in front of their families "while listening to music."

Five "subversives" were killed in Chalatenango. One was a woman.

A Treasury Police patrol was attacked in Guajoyo. Two agents were wounded.

Five hundred subversives attacked in Nuevo Eden.

The bodies of two brothers, 26 and 20 years old, were found in the El Cocal part of San Salvador. Both were decapitated.

The body of a 24-year-old was found in the road in El Angel. He had been shot in the eye and had a broken arm and leg.

In Usulután, a 24-year-old student was shot in front of his house.

Benedicto Sanchez, 28 years old, was taken from his home by masked men.

The body of Rafael Nerio was found with machete hacks and gunshots.

For April 30, 1981, the day after I was shot, there are no clippings related to the shooting. Perhaps the local media ignored it, or the chronicler of death decided it did not fit his narrative.

A photo of German Molina of Santa Emilia, Sonsonate, was published. He had been decapitated.

A large photo showed the caskets of three youths and an adult kidnapped and shot by masked men in Nejapa.

There was also a large photo of the two Nicaraguan fishermen, accused of being arms smugglers, who said they escaped the terror of Nicaragua to come to El Salvador.

If I had stayed for 10 days in El Salvador, this is what I would have found on the daily body rounds conducted by local and foreign media. I too would have taken photos without hesitation of the dead and decapitated bodies. This was El Salvador, not Woodland car crashes.

The Other Missing American

The disappearance and murder of Americans in El Salvador, I learned years after the fact, did not start with John Sullivan.

In fact, an American was arrested by Salvadoran military personnel in the fall of 1976 and then disappeared. Nobody seems to talk about him, and to my knowledge, he is referenced in only one book about the war, maybe because he was a Black American.

According to human rights reports, Ronald James Richardson was arrested for "vagrancy." The U.S. State Department, according to a report by journalist Karen DeYoung, was reluctant to get involved.

A telegram in December 1976 from the U.S. Embassy in El Salvador to the State Department was headlined with the words "possible assassination of AmCit Ronald James Richardson."

Embassy personnel met with then-president Arturo Molina and indicated they had information that Richardson had been killed by members of the Salvadoran immigration service with the knowledge of high-ranking military officers. Molina directed several of his top ministers to begin an investigation. The telegram said that one ranking Salvadoran diplomat admitted that Richardson had been killed by "security forces."

An American official stated in the cable, "I emphasized to the President my and the U.S. Government's wish that the matter be cleared up and appropriate action taken before possible public disclosure and inquiry into the case occurred."

But later the State Department sent a cable to the Embassy stating, "Richardson had been 'eliminated' by the Salvadoran security service after his arrest because 'they did not know what to do with him.'"

The U.S. government said Richardson entered El Salvador on August 25 and claimed he wanted to fight as a mercenary for the Salvadoran government. Salvadoran officials later claimed he had been deported to Guatemala, though he never was seen again.

In her memoir of her time in El Salvador, *What You Have Heard Is True*, poet Carolyn Forche describes being visited by a human rights activist who related to her that Richardson and several other political prisoners were put in a military helicopter and "tossed alive" into the Pacific Ocean. He told her at the time, "If a Salvadoran officer can kill an American without the United States government investigating the murder or changing its policy toward the [Salvadoran] government, then that means anyone can be killed in El Salvador."

I only discovered the Richardson story in 2023, after reading Forche's book. It struck me as an unsettling preview of how the disappearance and murder of American citizens would be handled in the future by the State Department, its Salvadoran Embassy, and the Salvadoran government and military.

The Ace of San Salvador

When I reached out to John Newhagen, the former UPI chief in El Salvador, in 2022, I hoped he might remember the shooting and that he would have more information about Gilberto—where he had come from, where his family had lived and might be living now. But when I called, he was not sure who I was. We had met in the hallway of the Camino Real on my first day in San Salvador, when he had made it clear that the *Daily Democrat*'s subscription to UPI wire photos did not earn me any special dispensation to get his help. My experience had not been unique. Freelancers who needed help were everywhere.

But Newhagen—who, when we talked, was working as a professor of journalism at the University of Maryland—did remember the excitement of running a bureau in the middle of a war. "The UPI was the first to open an office in San Salvador," he said from his home in upstate Maryland. "The Camino Real was the real press center."

Freelancers were the lifeblood of the wire services, serving up photos and stories. "A lot of the freelancers made a living not because they were competent but because they were crazy and exposed themselves," Newhagen recalled. Of course, the big guns were there too. The best war photographers in the world prowled the streets of El Salvador: John Hoagland for *Time*, Robert Nickelsberg and Susan Meiselas. The *Los Angeles Times* sent their veteran "fireman" Dial Torgerson, while *The Washington Post* had Christopher Dickey and Alma Guiller-moprieto. And the most respected were Raymond Bonner and Alan Riding, of *The New York Times*.

Newhagen himself had been in and out of Central America since the late '60s. He was a Navy veteran who served in the Caribbean in 1965. Like a lot of young Americans during the cultural tumult of the '60s, Newhagen had the fresh journal-istic spirit. "When I was an undergraduate in college, I met a bunch of guys in 1967 who were headed south. I jumped in the back of a Chevy station wagon and we set out to see if we could make it to Panama and back during spring break."

He went on to work on a railroad in Colorado and then kicked around Latin America throughout the late '60s and early '70s. In 1976, he spent a year in Costa Rica studying at the National University, and it was there that he met members of the San-dinista movement that had overthrown the repressive Somoza regime in Nicaragua in 1979.

He remembers the killing of American TV reporter Bill Stew-art in Nicaragua in 1979 as a kind of lightning-rod event, say-ing, "It accelerated what I was doing, what my plans were." Stewart worked for NBC news and was executed on camera by members of the Somoza military. It was a turning point in U.S. support for the Somoza family, which, like other Latin cau-dillos, had ruthlessly ruled Nicaragua for three generations. Newhagen went to work for an English-language newspaper in

Costa Rica. The week after the Somoza regime fell, Newhagen was in Managua witnessing one of the first true revolutions in Latin America since Cuba had fallen to Castro in 1959.

In the parlance of the trade, Newhagen had "strings" going in 1979 and 1980. These are informal arrangements with newspapers big and small, news services, and anybody who would buy a story or a photo. It is perhaps the most exciting aspect of journalism and its least rewarding in terms of compensation. It is the backbone of how news and information were spread around the globe in an efficient and frugal manner.

At one point, Newhagen was the only full-time correspondent in Guatemala when then-president Gen. Fernando Romeo Lucas Garcia began the extermination of opponents and indigenous peoples. His strings included *BusinessWeek* and the *Miami Herald*. A typical payment would be $400 for a story that could land him on a death list. "That was okay," he recalled.

But his best job, he said, was his first full-time job. He was hired by Juan Tamayo to be the UPI bureau chief in El Salvador early in 1981, just a few months before I arrived. Newhagen would become a legend in San Salvador, not only for the amount of copy he would generate, but for his knowledge of the area, his contacts, and his commitment to getting the story out.

Everywhere in the world, there is a first-class hotel where journalists stay during a war. In El Salvador, it was the Camino Real. When Newhagen set up shop there, he made clear, he was not "going from luxury hotel to luxury hotel. I was riding the chicken buses." He added, "I knew the terrain. I spoke

Spanish well enough to know what was going on. It was my shot at the big time, and I wanted to do a good job. It was a 24/7 deal." While Newhagen had an apartment that was "home," not far from the hotel, his office, his darkroom, and his tele-type machine were all in the Camino Real. He worked out of a backpack and would spend up to a week at a time sleeping in a hammock in the hotel room. (One reporter who worked in El Salvador later described Newhagen this way: "Many reporters came to El Salvador sane and, after all the killing, left insane. John Newhagen came insane and left insane.")

At the time, "the level of conflict was so intense there were no tourists. The hotels were empty." The civilian death count that year was the highest of the entire war. Bodies of death-squad victims were routinely dropped in the parking lot of the Cami-no Real to receive maximum coverage in the media.

The Camino Real itself could be dangerous. Newhagen recalled how the bomb set off by the guerrillas at an office building across from the hotel blew out the glass in his office. According to legend, the NBC office pet parrot was blown clear out of its cage. In declassified U.S. State Department cables, there is the story of the Salvadoran National Guard invading the Camino Real and searching the offices and rooms of journalists. When U.S. Embassy officials arrived, they found Newhagen on the phone to his Mexico City editors chronicling the search. Even the U.S. Embassy saw the search as harass-ment. They only confiscated items: two police scanners.

But what scared journalists and Salvadorans alike the most were the death squads.

At the time, the Reagan Administration and the Salvadoran government disavowed any knowledge of the death squads, but on the streets of El Salvador, it was pretty clear that the death squads operated with the approval of the government and the military. How else could they operate all night with a military-controlled curfew in place? Declassified documents later showed that U.S. officials knew the death squads' funders and origins. But they believed that if they went after the death squads, it would undermine the shaky military and even shakier government. "It was thought they operated throughout Central America at the time," Newhagen observed. "In Salvador, that they were directly connected to the military and military intelligence, or with thugs working with [military] blessing."

Newhagen, however, believed it was more complicated: He thought that certain elements of the military did not condone the death squads but were powerless to control them. The leader of the military, Gen. Jose Guillermo Garcia, knew the death squads were operating and who was behind them, "but he also knew who was buttering his bread." The worst thugs, Newhagen recalled, were the Treasury Police.

Looking back to El Salvador's most bloody time, when he was the chronicler for one of the most widely distributed news services in the world, he believes that "the higher questions of right and wrong didn't make a lot of sense. It was the existentialism of pain. It didn't matter how it was done or who it was done to; it was just being done."

He did not much believe in folks like me who felt that the world needed to be shown the atrocities of the U.S. government's puppets in San Salvador. "I was down there too long. I had seen enough. When people came down with a chip on their shoulder and try to explain why one side was right and the other side was wrong, it just seemed we were beyond that. Moralizing wasn't a useful exercise."

John Newhagen didn't remember my shooting, though he'd taken a photo of me in the Policlínica hospital in San Salvador. More disappointing for my quest, he knew nothing about Gilberto Moran. Nor did he remember that, after I'd been shot, he'd grabbed my camera and developed all the film inside. He handed me back the negs with the news that there weren't any shots worth printing and sending out. His shot of me bleeding from wounds in the hands and shoulder, on the other hand, went around the world.

The reality was that there was too much blood, death, and mayhem for him to track. I was a reporter who would not last long. He was holding down the most dangerous assignment in the world.

At the Miami Herald

The search for Gilberto at some point had to lead to Miami. The *Miami Herald* was one of the most comprehensive chroniclers of Central America. Its staff included some of the best reporters who had spent time covering the war in El Salvador. Despite the fact that a hurricane was predicted to hit during my stay, I had to talk to these critical sources. They might have seen or heard something. They might hold an important key to my search.

When I first reached out to Juan Tamayo, the former UPI Mexico City bureau chief who had been reporting from El Salvador in the 1980s, he seemed preoccupied. His current position was chief of foreign correspondents for the *Miami Herald*. Those correspondents were all in Latin America. But he agreed to an interview, and he met me in his office at the *Herald*'s imposing monolith of a building on a Friday morning in October 2005.

Perched on a spectacular piece of land along Biscayne Bay, the *Miami Herald* was considered one of the 10 best papers in the U.S. and was run by Knight-Ridder, a newspaper company that during the '80s and '90s was considered one of the bright spots in American corporate journalism.

Tamayo met me in the grand but largely empty lobby, where only a few weeks earlier a Miami city councilmember had pulled out a gun while on the phone with a *Herald* reporter and fatally shot himself in the head.

I expected a gruff, self-important "professional" journalist, but what I encountered was a soft-spoken, grandfatherly intellectual. He was dressed as I would dress: jeans, comfortable shirt, no sign of tie ligatures on his neck. I'd showed up more than an hour early, but he apologized to me for running "behind."

I sat in a sparse waiting room outside the sprawling *Herald* newsroom as he prepared for the 11 a.m. news meeting. Hurricane Wilma, bearing down on Florida, had disrupted all the traditional journalism schedules, and he had to figure out what news would run in the Sunday paper.

When Tamayo returned, he took me to the *Herald*'s staff cafeteria, with huge picture windows looking out on the Mac-

Arthur Causeway over Biscayne Bay out to the high rises of Miami Beach.

Like his former colleague Newhagen, Juan Tamayo didn't remember me.

And he didn't remember the piece he had written after my shooting that was critical of freelancers, including me. I had thought I would confront him about it—about what I saw as the values and the freedom of freelance journalism, and about the sharp needle he used toward me, throwing me in with prima donnas and fakers, failing to mention the months of preparation and planning that had preceded my trip.

But now that I was with him in person, I recognized him as a principled journalist who had faced death for far longer than a few days in El Salvador. He was on the widely circulated list of reporters who were threatened by the death squads. His failure to remember me reinforced the realization that I was not a big deal, that my shooting was a blip in the history books, and that the bigger story needed experienced journalists with a powerful newspaper platform.

I didn't explain what his criticism had meant to me, how it had stung. Instead, we talked about his life as a journalist and how El Salvador had only been a small part of a career that spanned the continents, from Mexico to Berlin to Jerusalem and, more recently, Baghdad.

Tamayo was born in Cuba in 1948. He came to the U.S. when he was 13. His parents were from the "middle, middle class," and the family had what he described as "a fairly normal American life." His father worked as a traveling rep for an

American pharmaceutical company. He grew up in Bridgeport, Connecticut, and while there were a few other Cubans
there, there was not the south-looking fervor that Cubans had
in Miami. "Latin America was a distant sort of thing," he
recalled.

That changed for him, he said, after he received a fellowship
from the Inter American Press Association right out of journalism school at Marquette University. The fellowship took
him to Buenos Aires for a year between 1971 and 1972. The
year "sealed the idea" of journalism as a profession and Latin
America as a specialty.

He returned to Bridgeport to work as a reporter for a local
paper and quickly moved after two years to the UPI bureau in
Hartford. He was moved to the UPI international desk in New
York in 1976. In early 1979, he was moved to Mexico City, but
he had already covered the Sandinista uprising in Nicaragua
in 1977 and the Castro regime in Cuba in 1978.

When Tamayo arrived, Mexico City was the hub for the world
coverage of Latin America. All the major U.S. and foreign
news organizations had their bureau chiefs in Mexico City.
In those days, almost all the stringers working for UPI were
Spanish-speaking locals in each country. But the need expand-
ed as the region heated up, and the Reagan Administration
declared that Central America would be the battleground in
the Cold War against the Soviet Union.

Even for those who worked in Guatemala, where the military
was running amok in the countryside; or Nicaragua, where
Reagan had started a secret war to overthrow the Sandinistas;
or Colombia, where the drug cartels were just starting their

massive export of large quantities of cocaine north, El Salvador was something different.

"There was definitely a sense it was not a normal situation," Tamayo said. "Around the corner from our office, a photographer had been shot and killed. There was a sense that the media was not being respected by the government and the death squads. In fact, they saw foreign press as agents of the guerrillas and the communists."

Another legendary reporter based in El Salvador in the early 1980s was Juan Vasquez, who worked with Tamayo at the *Miami Herald* and held the position of deputy editorial page editor. In 1981, Vasquez was a foreign correspondent for the *Los Angeles Times*, another of the most powerful and influential papers in the U.S.

Vasquez was at the *Herald* the day I met Tamayo, and I asked if we could be introduced. I had caught him by surprise, but he quickly agreed to an interview the next day, a Saturday. He looked at me with some puzzlement after I had been introduced by Tamayo. "Your name is familiar," he said. I explained I had been shot. "I remember. You were from Northern California. I remember that shooting," he said.

The next day, Vasquez and I met back at the *Herald* building. The place was empty, and I was a little surprised. I had always pictured a big newsroom like the *Herald*'s as constantly buzzing, particularly with a big hurricane coming in. But other than a pair of women in one cubicle and some press operators going home, the place was empty.

On the wall of Vasquez's office, a map of the world filled one whole wall. He was in to proofread editorials because the paper planned to shut down on Monday, the day Hurricane Wilma was scheduled to hit Miami after slamming into the west coast of Florida.

"I'm sure I was in town the day you were shot," Vasquez said right away. "Last night, I tried to find my notes from that day, but I don't have them. I'm sure I heard of this from Manny [Alvarez], but I didn't write about it."

At this point, Vasquez seemed almost apologetic, realizing that here was a California reporter who had nearly been killed, and Vasquez, as a reporter for the most important paper in California, the *Los Angeles Times*, had missed the story. "I was working on something else and I asked the desk if they wanted something, but Newhagen said he was going to move something. I remember the incident. I remember the interpreter."

Vasquez had grown up in Texas along the Mexican border. His deep Mexican-American roots led to troubles later in El Salvador, where Mexicans were viewed with suspicion, if not outright hostility.

A University of Texas journalism major, Vasquez had originally been interested in TV news. He traces his path to El Salvador back to a stint as the city editor for the *San Antonio Express-News*. The *Los Angeles Times*, desperate for Latino editors and reporters, recruited him from there in late 1979 as an assistant metropolitan editor. No more than eight months later, he was asked if he wanted to go to Central America as a reporter without portfolio. It was a unique opportunity that Vasquez took advantage of.

Vasquez went into El Salvador in mid-1980 with no phone numbers, no contacts, and no sources. Why, I asked, would he drop off the ladder to the editor's chair at the *Times* and take on a risky assignment far from the center of power?

"I liked to write. I had already decided that being an assistant metro editor wasn't what I wanted. I didn't enjoy it. I wanted to write." He gave words to my own dreams of always being able to return to writing.

Nicaragua was Vasquez's first stop. He wrote two or three stories from there, the long multi-jump stories that the *Los Angeles Times* was famous for in the '80s and into the '90s. He then moved on to El Salvador and the Camino Real Hotel.

He remembers there only being two other journalists there covering the war. One was Alfonso Rojo, a Spaniard; the other was Ian Mates, the South African cameraman who was killed a few months later after the car he was in hit a land mine.

"They saw me at breakfast and came over. Ian said, 'You must be a hack. We're the only journalists in town.' So, I spent a day with them. They took me around. We did the daily body count."

At some point, every American journalist who spent real time in El Salvador did the daily body count. You would drive from morgue to morgue or funeral home to funeral home. You would stop by El Playón and see if any bodies had been dumped there at the volcano. It was the route into the underworld of Salvadoran violence and horror.

Every reporter I know who worked in El Salvador has stories of close calls, of soldiers pointing guns at them, and of precarious escapes. Vasquez was no exception. "At first I was so scared," he said. "But you get hurt when you get careless. A lot of times it was because you were in the wrong place at the wrong time." For example, Vasquez remembered in 1988 being at a particular place during a guerrilla offensive and then learning that a British journalist had been killed by a sniper the very next day at the very same spot.

Being a Latino and fluent in Spanish, Vasquez said, made it easier to blend in. He could walk the streets with some level of confidence. But soldiers were suspicious of him if they heard his Mexican-American accent. One time, while racing to cover a press conference at the ambassador's home in the tony San Benito district, Vasquez made a left turn even though a sign prohibited it. Out of nowhere, a soldier appeared, pointing a big clumsy rifle at Vasquez. "I got out of the car, waved my passport, and told him I was an American," Vasquez related. "He said, 'You're a Mexican.'" Vasquez argued with the soldier, who could not understand how a "Mexican" could also be an American. Finally, he was allowed to go.

When Vasquez made it to the ambassador's residence, the American guard pointed at his shirt and wanted to know what had happened. Vasquez's shirt was soaked with sweat, and he recalled it had the "smell of fear."

Reporters like Vasquez were the official record-keepers of the official statements, even if sometimes the statements were bizarre.

No freelancer could ever get in to see the Salvadoran generals, but Vasquez recalled he did not have trouble setting up an interview with Gen. Jose Guillermo Garcia, then the head of the armed forces. It was around the same time as the press conference I had attended with Garcia and National Guard commander Gen. Carlos Eugenio Vides Casanova, who had talked about how the country was generally very peaceful with only a few problems. This was a common theme in the early '80s, when the violence being perpetrated by the death squads was reaching a crescendo and the guerrillas had turned the Salvadoran military into a garrison-bound fighting force.

Vasquez recalled that a fellow reporter had tagged along to his interview with Garcia. Garcia assured the two reporters that the fighting was all the result of "delinquents" and common criminals. These *"delincuentes"* called themselves guerrillas because it sounded romantic, Garcia said.

When Vasquez's companion asked Garcia if it was true that Garcia was running the death squads, Vasquez said he almost died on the spot. But Garcia laughed and said he knew nothing about any death squads.

Outside, a furious Vasquez asked why the reporter had asked such a provocative question, one that could have led to repercussions against both of them. The answer: "Because I'm out of here on a six o'clock flight."

It was a reminder of the self-imposed restrictions reporters had when addressing the fact that the military was clearly running death squads that were brutally killing Salvadorans from all walks of life.

"Salvador was difficult for me," Vasquez admitted. "It was so grim. My recollections of seeing so many dead bodies in so many places. The stark black-and-white nature of it. It was surreal in a way."

When Vasquez made it to Perquín, a far northern town where the FMLN had taken over the city and was running it as a rebel "zone," he recalled, it looked like something out of a Western movie. Every building was riddled with bullets. Many had been bombed out. Yet rural life went on and American reporters came, photographed, and interviewed. Then they headed back to San Salvador, the Camino Real, and a military that said that it was delinquents they were fighting.

Vasquez seemed conflicted about how much responsibility the U.S. should take for the killing in El Salvador and its dire poverty. On the one hand, he noted Reagan had called El Salvador "our backyard," and yet when the Cold War ended, it not only was not our backyard—it was not even in the same neighborhood. "We walked away," Vasquez said.

Even worse, we "neglected" Nicaragua, where we waged a secret and bloody war to overthrow a popular government we didn't like. But the personal feeling that so many correspondents and freelancers felt at one point about this war seemed best summarized toward the end of our interview. In El Salvador, he said, the "bizarre became commonplace."

Neither Tamayo nor Vasquez had new information to give me about my shooting. Nor did they have any leads on what had happened to Gilberto, Steve Patten, or the CBS crew. When I left the huge, hulking *Miami Herald*, a powerful yet ever-weakening purveyor of fact and opinion, I realized I had not gotten what I came for. But I got other things: the sense that we were all scarred by the mixture of death and close calls we'd seen and encountered, as well as a reminder that, during this awful time in American and Salvadoran history, none of us felt we had done that much about it. Nor, we knew, was the U.S. doing much today.

Living Dangerously

Death during the civil war in El Salvador was ubiquitous and unpredictable. It could come from a misplaced land mine or a trigger-happy checkpoint guard. It could come from a sniper or a death-squad operation. For Salvadorans, it had become their way of life. For journalists, it was being in the wrong place at the wrong time.

In such circumstances, it is not surprising that the American and European reporters quickly found themselves a brothel to hang out in. References to the use of sex workers by American correspondents, like references to the widespread use of marijuana and occasional use of cocaine, have been sparse. Nobody at the time wanted to expose the journalists, and nobody later wanted to embarrass them.

In at least one case, a well-known journalist married a sex worker.

Viviana Moreno, whom I met in Miami on my trip to see Juan Tamayo, was a photographer who turned into a respected "fixer," or the person who set up interviews, made logistical arrangements for travel into war zones, and generally tried to keep her clients alive. I met her at one of Miami's major shopping malls, and she talked openly about "La Casa de Gloria."

Moreno couldn't remember where it had been located, though she said it was only 20 minutes from the Camino Real, but she called it "very famous." It was where Americans went to hang out with sex workers, buy their services, and spend the night if the 7 p.m. curfew came before they had finished their business.

It was also a place, Moreno said, where reporters could "go to gossip." There were Americans from the embassy, Americans from the military, and lots of other reporters to pass along tips and leads. She said it was mostly for print people, those who needed a depth of information and the context of the crazy war being fought outside their hotel rooms. "You would hear if there was an operation in a certain area," she recalled. "We would know the day before. You would hear if an area was hot. The boys would talk to us, and everything was off the record."

Moreno went there often. Her companion and chaperone was John Hoagland, who would later be killed in a firefight while shooting photos for *Newsweek*.

"We would stay all night, talking bullshit, not sleeping, going home in the morning because of the curfew," she said. Then, as was custom, the group would make its tour of dumping grounds to do the body count, or as Moreno described it, "doing the body dumps."

The ritual, she said with a smile, was "considered living dangerously." She emphasized that it was undertaken by the foreign press, not the locals. "The local photographers, they had family. They didn't want to find them one morning."

TV reporters and cameramen would not participate because there was no way they could put the never-ending carnage on U.S. TV screens. But the still photographers knew they could shoot the angles just right so that they would appear, if not in American magazines, in European pictorials.

Argentinian-born, Moreno had come to El Salvador as an idealistic still photographer with a Konica camera. (I too carried a Konica. It was like driving onto a professional racetrack in the South in a Kia. The pros all carried Nikons. The cost of their lenses alone could feed a Salvadoran family for years.)

But Moreno understood how to be at the right place at the right time, and she knew what angle to take.

"All my life, I had wanted to take pictures," she said. "My grandparents had given me a camera for my 15th birthday, and since then I have wanted to take pictures."

In 1980, she had gone to New York and then to San Francisco to try and break into photography. She quickly encountered the old journalistic refrains: Don't bother applying if you don't have experience; nobody here will give you that experience. Later that year, in Los Angeles, she spoke to the *Los Angeles Times* and then the *Chicago Tribune*. No luck.

United Press International, however, was interested. They had a strong photo wire and suggested she be a stringer based in Mexico City. Juan Tamayo offered her the job, and "Being young and stupid, I said yes."

In early 1981, shortly after the murder of the American nuns along the road from the airport to the hotels, she was sent to El Salvador. "They told us not to take the bus from the airport. They said to take a helicopter."

She was traveling with Alicia Casal, an old Argentinian friend, who had planned to simply drop Moreno in El Salvador and get out. On Casal's first night at the Camino Real, however, she met John Newhagen and never left. Today, she and Newhagen are married and have a family.

Moreno and Casal had a little apartment behind the Camino Real. "The idea was for me to work there for two or three months, get a name, and then go on. I stayed until the end of 1982," Moreno recalled.

Moreno and Newhagen worked together closely. "John and I lived dangerously," she said, noting that print photographers would often go where TV cameramen refused to go. "The TV people would always have their cooler in their van, head out and shoot the bang bang, then take out their cold drinks and sandwiches."

On a small budget, earning $20 a photo from UPI and $40 a photo from AP, Moreno dreamed of buying a Nikon. Later, the dream got bigger and included a Leica. Unlike the big-name journalists, she had no driver or helper. She often took public buses to the scenes of incidents.

Moreno's drive to get new equipment quickly led her to more lucrative work: setting up shots and helping coordinate TV crews, particularly ones that flew in from the U.S. with no background and no experience. Now she was making $200 a day, a queenly sum in El Salvador.

Moreno vividly remembered the massacre in Soyapango in late March 1981. Like most of the journalists there, she had heard the news at the hotel. "It was the first massacre I went to. It was horrible." Moreno said she recalled the small street where the journalists were directed. "There were literally bodies all over the street. They were still in their underwear.

I remember the color of the bodies. It was waxy. They were waxy-looking in their underwear. You remember that forever. There was a young man among them. I was 22. I thought it could have been me."

On April 29, she said, she remembers having heard about the shooting of Joaquin Zuniga in Soyapango, but nothing about Gilberto or me. She had no idea who Steve Patten was.

El Salvador was a dangerous place for everybody.

On one occasion, while Moreno was riding a bus to take photographs for a story, the bus hit a mine and flipped over. Several people on the bus were killed. Moreno suffered a dislocated jaw. "An angel was flapping over me," she said. When she got back to San Salvador, one of the veterans of the Salvadoran foreign press corps told her not to go back into the countryside.

But later in 1981, she returned to Morazán province, where fighting was particularly heavy. She wanted to go out with the soldiers on a patrol—"I think Newhagen told me we needed more soldier photos"—and after cajoling and wheedling the local commander for hours, she was finally told to get in one of a convoy of trucks, but to sit up in the cab, considered the safest place. "I was in a competition with Newhagen that day to see which one of us would get out on a patrol first," she recalled.

The soldiers told her not to get out of the truck unless she was given the okay. Her truck was the second in the convoy.

Two miles outside of Morazán, mines on both sides of the road suddenly detonated in the middle of the convoy. She remembers watching the truck in front of her disappear in an explosion and cloud of smoke. Inside her truck, three soldiers were dead and one had lost his leg. Her ear and arm were hit by shrapnel. Nearby, a young soldier lay beside the road with his leg blown off. A medic raced from wounded soldier to wounded soldier, his pants laced with morphine needles. When the medic ran out of medical tape, he began using duct tape to bind wounds. All the while, Moreno was shooting photos.

When she returned to San Salvador, one of the veterans told her, "You are pulling the devil's tail. Eventually he will get back at you."

But Moreno was fierce. "Yes, they told me not to go back, but then they wanted me to tell them all about the battle in great detail so they could file stories."

"I was a woman trying to break into a man's world. At one point, they [the men] said I was okay, 'She is one of us.' That was a great compliment. But it was not that I was okay, but that I was one of them."

Later, she broke her foot while jumping into a ditch during an ambush near Usulután.

For Moreno, El Salvador was never the stepping stone to prominence as a war photographer. She was in it, she said, "Not for the bang-bang photos, but for the photo of the boy in the refugee camp whose eyes would melt your heart."

Today, Moreno has three Leicas. She has shot the wars in the Falklands and in Iraq. She shot the fall of the Soviet Union and the Contras war out of Honduras.

I asked her about her politics, both before and after the war. She did not talk about left or right, but rather her firm belief that "people should have an opportunity to develop to their potential."

Moreno's husband, Roberto Morceno, joined us for part of our conversation. They met in El Salvador, where he had worked for the networks. They later married and traveled to the world's hot spots as a team. Even though Morceno knew all the teams in El Salvador, he could not remember Steve Patten or his crew either, though he gave me a half-dozen others to call. It was a strange dead end, with no new information about the CBS crew, let alone Gilberto. But I had a new list of names to track down. And these people, too, had stories to tell.

Manny Alvarez, the Wild Man

By the time I was gearing up for my trip to Miami, my search was well into its sixth year and I still had no leads on where Gilberto Moran was buried or what happened to his family. Steve Patten and his CBS TV crew had seemingly disappeared after their Salvador stint. Phone call after phone call failed to turn up anybody who could even remember the crew, let alone tell me how to find them.

But I continued using the time-tested journalistic phone-tree methodology. Call one person and ask for three or four names of others. Run through old newspaper files and call reporters whose bylines were listed. Keep calling people, keep filling up notebooks with names and numbers.

I was making some progress in tracking down those who had worked and lived in El Salvador in the early '80s, but few people remembered me, Patten, or Moran. It was like we had ghost-walked through a war zone.

So it was a shock when I called Manny Alvarez, a videographer who had worked in El Salvador in the early '80s, and the first words out of his mouth were: "I remember you. You were shot down there."

I had obtained Alvarez's name from Juan Tamayo when I was setting up my interview with him in Miami. He did not have Alvarez's phone number, but he gave me the name of somebody who did. When I called Alvarez, he instantly knew me. "It was like it was yesterday," he recalled.

Not only did Alvarez remember me, he said, but he had filmed me as I was loaded into the ambulance. His footage ended up on NBC news the night of the shooting, with correspondent Jim Cummins narrating the piece.

Alvarez, like Tamayo, Vasquez, and Moreno, lives in Miami. From generals to journalists, Miami seems to have attracted all of Latin America's refugees and renegades. It is as Latin as any South or Central American capital, boasting a Little Havana as well as a host of branch offices for the biggest banks in Latin America.

When I flew down to talk with these former foreign correspondents, Alvarez had just returned from Africa, where he was filming the war in the Congo. He welcomed me into his sprawling suburban home, his suitcase from the trip still sitting on the living room floor, dirty clothes still wrapped in the tight rolls of a journalist who knows how to pack as much underwear as can fit in any small space.

El Salvador, Alvarez told me, was the defining moment in his life and his career. To this day, he points to his experiences there as what would eventually lead him all over the world, from the Falklands war to the Panama invasion to the Gulf War.

Like many Miamians, Alvarez is the son of Cuban refugees. His parents brought him to South Florida in 1960. He was three years old. They landed in Hialeah, where almost all the kids were Cuban and almost all the families spoke Spanish. "My parents bought a house in Hialeah for $14,000. It was an agricultural area with cows behind the school buildings."

Alvarez liked hanging out with the Cuban kids, because unlike the gringos in his neighborhood, the Cubans liked cool music, and they liked getting to know girls. He wanted to be a disco deejay, while his practical, immigrant father wanted him to go to college and major in business.

In Alvarez's first semester at Miami Dade Community College, he received an F in accounting. That ended the expectations for a business career. But the campus had communication courses. "It had a radio-broadcasting program. I fell in love with it. A light bulb went off."

His radio courses at college helped win him a low-level gofer job on the local WPLG, where he learned how to haul TV cable around the newsroom, run cameras, and put on a TV news show. When a cameraman's job opened at a competitor, a CBS affiliate, Alvarez grabbed it.

There he met many of the CBS correspondents who would be moving in and out of Latin America. The Miami bureau for CBS was located in the same offices as the radio station, so it was natural that local and national news crews would get to know each other.

One of the first big stories he worked was the 1980 Mariel boatlift, when Fidel Castro emptied his jails and prisons, loaded the occupants on boats, and sent them to the U.S., where they were welcomed by the anti-Castro refugee community as heroes. Only later would many Americans realize that Castro had hoodwinked the U.S. government into taking his most undesirable citizens. The boatlift brought more than 125,000 Cubans to Florida.

That same year, at the age of 23, Alvarez, intrigued by the war stories of the foreign correspondents, decided to quit the local affiliate and go to El Salvador. There he worked for Bernie Nudelman, who had his own production company sending film and stories back to NBC.

"I was a kid, and I knew nothing about El Salvador," Alvarez recalled.

His first trip there was on a Learjet, which NBC used to fly crews in and out of El Salvador. His jarring welcome to the country came when a Salvadoran soldier asked him what he was wearing under his jacket. "I told him it was a bulletproof vest." That was the last he ever saw of the vest.

He went on to shoot footage of workers cutting grass with machetes, but within hours, he was at the morgue. Outside, there was a sprawling pile of bodies, as though they had been dumped from the back of a truck. No dignity, no privacy, just bodies tossed like trash in the street.

"That was my first look at the violence. I filmed it. I had seen car accidents, and I had filmed ocean drownings. But I had never seen anything like that. They were just dumped there."

The routine for camera crews was pretty set. Crews would be in El Salvador for three to five weeks, then rotate out for rest. The networks paid well in a country where rent, food, and helpers were inexpensive. "I was making a lot of money. I worked hard and partied hard. When I went out in the morning, I didn't know if I was going to make at it back at night.

"When we got in, everybody headed for the bar. We partied until we passed out."

The Camino Real was "the lap of luxury" for the young man. "You could buy drugs; you could buy hookers. I was a kid in a candy store."

The young reporters leaned on the older reporters, people like Nudelman and Bernie Dietrich, to not only teach them journalism but also keep them out of trouble. "They would give you tips like, when you drove down a country road, you kept the door open in case you hit a land mine. The open door kept you from dying from the concussion inside the van," Alvarez said.

He began to realize that this was a country where there were no rules about life and death. "I had no idea that a power could come into your house, kill everybody in it, and nobody would do anything about it. There were no rules down there. The only rules were to listen to the older guys. They were the rules.

Your ticket to survival was listening to the older guys."

But it was also hard not to feel impervious and even above the violence. "I remember being in the Camino Real when a bomb went off across the street. We ran right over to it. When we got there, we could see it was a car bomb and a guy passing on a motorcycle had been killed. The bomb blew the guy apart. We found a foot in a tree.

"I remember asking one of the other TV guys how they were going to get that on TV back home."

Suddenly, another explosion ripped the area. A second bomb had been planted at the scene to go off when soldiers and police arrived at the first explosion. "The blow hit me in the head, and I thought I had been hit. I put my hand up to my head, but it had only been the force of the air hitting me."

Just as I relied on Gilberto Moran, Alvarez came to rely on his driver, Nelson Flores Ayala. "We became very, very close friends," Alvarez recalled. "I would go to dinner at his house, which had a dirt floor, and his wife would cook armadillo. They treated me like family. He saved my ass."

On one occasion, as Flores and Alvarez were driving across town, they spotted a soldier walking a prisoner across a field at gunpoint. Alvarez started to film the scene, and the soldier turned and pointed his gun at them, ready to shoot.

"The soldier then ran up to the car, and we all got down, got on the floor, except for Nelson. We thought the guy was going to shoot us, but Nelson talked him out of it.

"It was a young soldier, and he was shaking. Holding the gun. I think if it wouldn't have been for Nelson, that guy would have opened up on our van."

He added, "If the driver said we weren't going any farther, it didn't matter if the producer or the correspondent wanted to go further. We didn't go further."

In the middle of the interview, Alvarez's cell phone rang and he paused to answer. It was a local producer looking for a cameraman to film hurricane damage. "This is my dinner bell," explained Alvarez when the call ended. As a freelance videographer, when the phone rings—whether it's for a college football game or a war halfway around the world—the gear goes into the car, and Alvarez goes too.

First, however, we got around to talking about the day Gilberto and I were shot. Alvarez's memory, in contrast to almost everybody else I had interviewed, was vivid.

At the time, Alvarez had moved over to work for NBC. Nelson was with a crew from New York that had come down with national correspondent Jim Cummins, who was "big-footing" in El Salvador for a few days.

The call came into the hotel that there was a firefight in Soyapango. "I remember we went out, and when we got there, there was gunfire coming from everywhere. You couldn't tell where it was coming from.

"I remember there were little huts up and down the street and soldiers running around. People were scurrying in and out of their houses. They would step out of their houses, not freaked. You'd think they'd hide, but they would conduct their lives as usual.

"At some point, we hooked up with the CBS crew. They were putting on their bulletproof vests. To go around the corner. Nelson went over and joined them, but I thought it was a bad idea to go around a blind corner.

"That's when your guy [Gilberto] came over to me and said, 'Don't be a pussy.' He then went around that corner, and that was the last time I saw him alive."

It was the first time I had heard that Moran had disparaged one of the journalists. I distinctly remember journalists staying behind, particularly the crews from the Salvadoran TV station who had brought us to Soyapango. Had I been more experienced, I would have stayed with them. They knew. But for the first time, I was hearing that it may have been bravado at work when Gilberto told us it was safe to head around that corner. Of course, Zuniga would a few minutes later say it was safe. Patten seemed to think joining his crew would provide more safety.

Alvarez added, "Nelson, meanwhile, had joined my CBS pals and headed around the corner in the TV vans." Alvarez stayed behind.

"At some point, we were told that you guys had been shot," Alvarez continued. "We came in with the ambulance that had been called for you," he recalled. "We were dropped, and there were still gunshots. I remember we were dropped in a little culvert."

Joaquin Zuniga was lying on the ground, and a short distance away was Gilberto, lying motionless.

"The soldiers were pointing guns at us. They did not know if we were guerrillas. We were hiding in that culvert."

Later, Alvarez would remark, "The importance of that day was the CBS guys putting on the vests, but they didn't know anything about where they were going. For these guys, putting on the vests was meaningless. The Salvadorans had big FAL rifles that shot heavy rounds. You could be shot in the head." He pointed out that when the French photographer Olivier Rebbot had been shot in San Salvador three months earlier, the bulletproof vest he'd worn had not kept him safe from the round he took in the chest: He died in a Miami hospital three weeks later from his wounds.

Alvarez was more agitated as he continued. "Your guy [Moran] went in there blind. And then he told me I was a pussy. Then I looked at him and he was dead. What angel told me to not go down that road. What a weird place to be."

He added, "If I had caved in, then I might be lying there with him."

He still remembers when Father Roy Bourgeois "went missing" and how, for days, the press corps would search the morgues looking for his body. "I remember looking at a young, blue-eyed kid, blond, lying on the [morgue] slab with his eyes open. That was the first time I realized this could be me lying here. That scared the hell out of me." Going to the morgue and "looking at every white guy who came in" was "an activity so absurd as a human being. Now you know that, but then, it was what you did."

Then came what was, for me, the most powerful moment.

We moved into Alvarez's office, a typical journalist's junk

room and memory hall. On one wall was a bulletin board completely filled with press passes from around the world, from Haiti and Honduras to Peru and Ecuador. On another wall, the heads of four bucks were carefully mounted next to a raccoon in a playful pose. Stacks of film and tape filled the room, which was dominated by a huge TV screen surrounded by editing equipment.

Alvarez scanned through old shots of Miami riots and a beautiful introduction to El Salvador he had filmed a few days before my shooting. It includes nature shots and scenes from the Izalco volcano.

Up comes Tom Brokaw, announcing that journalists had been injured in El Salvador. There are shots of soldiers running and a long-distance shot of Gilberto Moran lying in the road. Steve Patten can be seen running at one point.

Then my face fills the screen as a man leans over me and wraps a tourniquet around my bleeding arm. I look dazed, in shock. Alvarez tells me the Good Samaritan is his driver, Nelson. I go from standing to sitting on the ground, then being led like a zombie into an ambulance.

Then it is over. It had lasted 60 seconds and taken me back 25 years. The road looks different than I remembered. What had seemed like a narrow culvert was in fact a wide part of the road shoulder. I had totally forgotten about Nelson putting that tourniquet on my arm. I certainly did not remember Manny Alvarez filming me.

My eyes, however, look just the way I remember feeling, and have never forgotten: filled with fear and uncertainty.

In the Wake of a Hurricane

After I did my interviews in Miami, Hurricane Wilma swept through and kept me in town for an extra three days.

I'd intended to ride it out from my perch in a Coconut Grove luxury hotel. But late in the day after the hurricane, the hotel still had no power, no phones, and dark hallways. Staff came to my door and said the hotel was closing. I was being "evacuated." My evacuation route took me by a $45 cab ride to an even swankier neighborhood along the Miami Beach condo canyons.

Sitting on the 15th floor, looking out at freighters backed up on the Atlantic Ocean and frolicking tourists in the emerald-green waters, I wondered what I was doing here.

It had been more than five years since I had begun this search, but I hadn't really gotten anywhere. I'd found no clues about where Gilberto was buried, could not locate Steve Patten or members of his crew. I had found the tape of my 60 seconds of fame, though I looked like a lost kid being led to safety by a brave ambulance crew. I was now paying $130 a night to wait for Miami International Airport to open and wondered if my kids would understand why that hadn't gone into their college fund. Though my wife, Denise Eschardies, put up with my quest, she wanted me home with her and our three kids. She had a sharp tone when I called to complain about life without electricity. As for my colleagues at the *Santa Barbara Independent*, where I was now the publisher, they figured I was a nutcase.

The year 2005 had opened with a trip to the urgent care clinic after my left arm had increasingly lost its strength and gone numb in various spots.

I wondered if it was the first sign of heart trouble, but a cardiologist said I had a great heart and should not be wasting his time. An internist said I needed high-blood-pressure medicine and to drop 30 pounds. But it was the trip to the X-ray lab that brought home my little pull on the "tail of the devil."

First came the X-ray of my elbow. There was the big chunk of lead, surrounded by three smaller, almost indistinct pieces. In my shoulder sat a bigger chunk, also surrounded by at least five other smaller pieces.

On the X-ray display screen, my shoulder and elbow bones were gray shadows, but the lead seemed almost to glow, like it was radioactive. I was now heading out for neurological tests and possibly a CAT scan to see what was happening to the muscles around those big chunks of shrapnel from 25 years before.

Perhaps the devil was playing catch-up. After all, my slow Rolodex search with multiple trips to El Salvador seemed to be making no progress. I could not find Moran's family, and nobody knew how to contact the CBS crew.

I could understand the lack of records in El Salvador, where chaos reigned. At least one foreign press veteran from that war marveled at how I had been able to get into the hall of records building in San Salvador at all, even though when I did, all I discovered was that they had no birth or death records for Gilberto Moran.

When I finished interviewing people on my hunt for answers, and my attempt to try to do something right, I liked to tell them that it was the search that was most important. But the search was going nowhere, and increasingly I was feeling like it was more an ego trip than a search. The pain and numbness in my left arm brought the realization that mortality might be catching up with me. Time might be running out.

Carrying the Casket

It was 2020, and I had ended my 32-year journalism career and taken a job at my alma mater, UC Santa Barbara. I was an assistant vice chancellor building a spectacular alumni house and raising money for scholarships. Among my tasks: meet and help cultivate and steward potential donors.

It was a donor dinner like so many before. Wealthy guests in a tony New York restaurant, but not too tony. Chancellor seated next to the big donor. Me off to the side, out of earshot.

Unknown to us, the COVID-19 virus was stealthily spreading throughout New York City, just outside the restaurant doors, perhaps just inside. We would only learn weeks later that the virus first exploded in New York City, and this was one of the last in-person donor visits either I or the chancellor would make.

Beth DeWoody was our host and a big philanthropist. She is the granddaughter of one of New York City's most success-ful real estate magnates and sits as the executive vice presi-dent of the company he founded, one that controls more real estate in the city than any other company. On the side, she runs the family foundation, and she is a big supporter of the arts. We were there to ask if she would be interested in supporting UCSB's Art Museum, a small but eclectic collection focusing on architecture and design.

DeWoody had brought her art buyer, a well-known, 60-something-year-old gallery owner named Craig Starr. As we chatted, Starr revealed he had once worked for CBS News in New York. Of course, my interest was piqued. "I've been trying to track down a colleague who worked at CBS in the early '80s," I said. "Do you know anybody there today who might be able to help me track him down?"

"What's his name?" Starr asked.

"Steve Patten," I responded.

He whipped out his cell phone, and at this point DeWoody became interested too. A detective story beat a handout request. "Here he is," said Starr, as I almost fell out of my chair. "He wrote a book called *Foreign Correspondent*." Sure enough, there was a photo of Steve Patten, balding head and all. I'm still not sure how I had never come across it before.

A new phase of my quest began.

I really did think I had searched everywhere for Steve Patten. I didn't know where he had escaped to when the bullets rained down. He showed up at the hospital the next day, and I saw him before I left the country. Then I had lost him.

Patten's autobiographical book, *Foreign Correspondent*, had been published in 2015 by an obscure printer named Lee & Grant International, where he had worked as an editor. His coauthor on the book was listed as Patricia Mosure.

The text told me the name of his cameraman, which I'd forgotten: Tony Foresta. I searched the internet and found he was the co-owner of a movie-camera dolly manufacturer along with his wife, Kaye Armstrong. Kaye Armstrong's social media site listed Steve as a friend. Another tipoff was a business card I had kept from CBS soundman Larry Bullard. It listed his employer as Flying Tiger Communications. Kaye Armstrong's LinkedIn profile indicated that in the '80s, she was the co-owner of Flying Tiger.

When I finally called Kaye at her home in DeLand, Florida, I thought I finally was going to find one of the most important pieces to the puzzle: Steve Patten's location. Kaye seemed outgoing and friendly, and when I asked almost immediately how I could get ahold of Steve, she replied, "He's dead. He died two years ago." It was as though a heavy metal door had just slammed shut. I had missed him.

Patten had kept a low profile, according to his book, because, while in Beirut, he had been accused of being a CIA operative. He was convinced that this was why CBS had fired him shortly after his El Salvador assignment. He was Republican, a Marine vet, and a supporter of Donald Trump. He spent the entire book trying to defend his reputation.

As for the El Salvador shooting, he devoted just three pages to it. But they gave me the lead I needed. He wrote that "hiring a young Salvadoran man as an interpreter" was among his "most profound regrets as a journalist." It was interesting to see the ways he kept me out of the story, and didn't mention that I hired Gilberto myself. I wondered if this was a way of protecting me. He wrote, of our experience, that "another journalist, my interpreter and I were walking down a road with a relatively high cliff to our left, and road-level bushes and shrubbery on our right." He wrote that the interpreter, whom I knew to be Gilberto, had reached into Steve's shoulder bag when the shots came. "The interpreter and the other journalist went down and I was pressed against the cliff to our left. The gunmen were apparently overhead firing from the top of the cliff down on us. I ran back in the direction from which we had come staying as close to the cliff as possible." Then he took shelter in a house a woman ushered him into.

"Later," the book continued, "when I went down the road I found the interpreter dead where he had been hit. The other journalist had been wounded and taken to a hospital. Tony and Larry were not far away, down the road on the other side."

Patten wrote:

> My interpreter's family was devastated. But they never blamed me, as they could have for the death of their beloved son and brother. I blamed me. I am so very sorry I led that young man to his death.

> They buried him in a beautiful hillside cemetery in a ceremony attended by his family and their friends. It was an overcast day and fog gently slipped down the hillside as I stood there watching the burial. I was the only journalist who was there to pay his or her respects. Except for one. Tony Foresta stood silently behind me for the entire ceremony. Only after it ended did he come up to me and ask if I was all right.

> I left El Salvador on May 3, 1981. Later on Tony told

me he heard the restaurant where we always ordered pizza had been blown up by the guerrillas. Or maybe by the government. Like with the murder of Archbishop Romero and the death of my interpreter, you never could be sure who was pulling the trigger.

Tony Foresta, Kaye's husband who was Patten's CBS soundman, filled in more of these scenes. Talking with him was like a family homecoming, but for a funeral, not a wedding. He recalled the shooting vividly.

"We came down the hill toward the power plant and met you and Steve as you were going down," he said. "I just felt like we were not in a good place. An army patrol came down the road. Regular army. I said if something happens, I want to be under their truck. We were filming the patrol coming up when the shit happened. The patrol was chasing people on the other side of the road and there was an ambush there. We knew Gilberto had been killed and the photographer hit in the sciatic nerve. That night, Larry and I visited you in the hospital, but you were in surgery, so we never saw you."

It was the next part of his recollection that grabbed me.

"Larry and I had run into Steve in El Salvador, and I just thought he was a good character. A stand-up kind of guy. When it came time to bury Gilberto, Steve and I went to the church and carried the casket out to the grave. It was a simple wood casket. I think Steve paid for it. Nobody from the press was there, and there were no family. I just thought that this kid [Gilberto] was working for the press. Some of them should have shown some respect."

Instead, he said, they were all at a "a volleyball game at the U.S. Marine House." The big-footer who had come in from CBS, he said, was also "very dismissive" of the idea of going to the funeral.

Where, I asked, was the church and cemetery? I needed to go there.

"I remember very little," Tony said. "It was in the country; there were no big buildings around. I just remember that I was worried there were not enough of us to carry the casket."

In 2023, I called Tony again to see if his memory had been jolted. It hadn't. Nobody from El Salvador has ever contacted him.

He sympathized with my search. For 20 years, he had tried to locate Larry Bullard. No luck. Larry had disappeared.

I could hear in Tony's voice the same undertone he had the first time he talked, when he asked what had happened to me. I had told him the embassy and press people said I should leave El Salvador immediately for my own safety. The doctors said I needed to go to the U.S. to have two big pieces of shrapnel taken out of my shoulder and elbow. I was not there to carry the casket.

But this time I told Tony, "Thank you. Thank you for what you did for Gilberto. Thank you for what you did for his family. And thank you for what you did for me. I appreciate it from the bottom of my heart."

He seemed to appreciate this after 40 years of silence.

He had done it because he was a journalist, and because he knew what was right.

Part III

From U.S. Bombs to Ecological Paradise

After more than two decades of searching, I have failed to find Gilberto Moran's gravesite, or his family. But I find myself pulled back to El Salvador again and again, now with a wider agenda. Over the course of my trips to find Gilberto, I had gradually become involved with a bigger mission: trying to bring medical help to the poorest areas of El Salvador. It wasn't going to help Gilberto's family directly, but perhaps I could try to chip away at the vast inequities between the Global North and South. Perhaps I could begin my own American restitution, as small as it would be. Like so many others before me, I had also been drawn to the beauty of the country and its amazing people.

I also wanted my children to experience El Salvador, and to understand what it meant about their history—both in terms of how it shaped me and, perhaps indirectly, our life as a family—as well as how they were implicated, as citizens of the U.S., in what had happened there.

So, in 2000, on my first trip back to El Salvador in 19 years, I took my stepdaughter, Kendra Casey, with me on a wide-ranging tour of the country. During my trip in 1981, I had wanted to head into the countryside, where the battles were fierce and the repression of campesinos particularly harsh. I never made it.

As we traveled from the airport to the Camino Real, I recalled a story I had written for *The Sacramento Bee* in May 1981—it covered the shooting, and included a description of the road from the airport to San Salvador: "It twists and turns through lush foliage and stunted coffee bushes that race up steep hillsides."

This wasn't just bad writing—it was bad reporting. The road was too low in altitude to support coffee trees, which are short but rarely stunted. The trees along that road were actually plain old jungle trees. It was an example of how little I knew

Driver "Che" and interpreter Kendra Casey in 2000. Photo by George Thurlow.

about El Salvador in 1981. On subsequent trips there, however, I visited coffee plantations and met the wealthy men and women who ran them.

Unlike me, Kendra was fluent in Spanish, and she was my interpreter as we spoke to everyone from FMLN legislators to campesinos in the countryside. The people we talked with across El Salvador seemed overwhelmingly gracious and generous. And it helped that Kendra has a sparkling personality. (She would later receive an advanced degree in Spanish literature.)

Through Leslie Schuld, the longtime director of the Salvador-based social justice organization Centro de Intercambio y Solidaridad (CIS), we were introduced to Guillermo Rivera, the charismatic mayor of Cinquera, a small town about three hours north of San Salvador. Schuld wanted Rivera's quest for Cinquera to become an ecological tourist spot to get publicity in the U.S. And she wanted me to get a taste of the war in the countryside, where Cinquera had been a constant Salvadoran military target. To get there, we first passed through another war-torn town: Suchitoto, where a monument to the war was placed in the town center. Then we traveled the rutted and butt-breaking road to Cinquera. When we arrived, there was not much to see. The house of the mayor, Guillermo Rivera, was the biggest and grandest. It was made of cement brick, not yet completed, and had an outhouse in the back jungle.

Rivera had been a guerrilla fighter during the war but now was the most powerful leader in the region. He was also very generous. He had invited us to come spend the night at his house and to join him and his family for dinner. He was filled with excitement about his new post-war dream: a nature preserve surrounding Cinquera, where ecotourists would come to see spectacular lake and mountain views, as well as the kitchen where the guerrillas cooked in the forest. Tourism, he hoped, would boost the local economy.

The mayor took us on a hike that he imagined would be the path for these future ecotourists. We were not gone long before we began to see the results of U.S.-supplied weaponry. The village's church had been bombed out, leaving only the façade. In front of the church were two bomb canisters. Nearby were the tail remains of a U.S. Huey helicopter. The intense aerial bombardment had come because of the nearby guerrilla camp of La Cascabel.

We walked into the jungle where the guerrillas had dug caves for their camp, and we passed old indigo processing ruins. (Indigo, which is also known by its Nahuatl word *xiquilite*, was once a huge economic treasure for El Salvador. In pre-

The casing of a 500-pound U.S.-supplied bomb dropped on the village of Cinquera. Photo by George Thurlow.

Conquest times, it was used to decorate ceramics and textiles. After the Spanish conquest of El Salvador, the Spaniards exported indigo because its rich blue dye was valued around the world. But when artificial dyes swept the clothing industry, indigo production died. Now it is harvested and processed as a boutique item and a tourist attraction.) We made it to the El Brujo falls and the idyllic El Salton pool. On our way home, we stopped at a village pineapple garden and harvested a pineapple.

We were prepared a rich dinner: an egg, beans, and as many homemade tortillas as we could eat. We had the pineapple for dessert after it was washed in tap water. My high level of paranoia gave way to common courtesy. The pineapple slices were incredibly sweet and delicious.

I was given the hammock in the spartan, unfinished room in front. Fortunately, I had a light to find my way to the outhouse. Soon before I went to bed, I asked, half-jokingly, "What time in the morning do the roosters start crowing?"

This was met by smiles and a few giggles. "You will see," Rivera said. About midnight, the first rooster started on the far edge of town. It was joined by another, then another. All night long, they crowed at each other, like dogs barking from one yard to another. Roosters start when they have something to crow.

The next day, on the bumpy, uncomfortable ride back to San Salvador, we learned the lesson many travelers before us have known: Don't drink the water, and don't eat pineapples rinsed in it. Kendra was horribly sick. When we got to the Alameda Hotel, the toilet and shower in our room were backed up. Maintenance workers were toiling as my stepdaughter got sicker. We gave up on our lodgings there and high-tailed it to the Camino Real, where Kendra slowly recovered. She had a new appreciation of high-end hotels, and I had a new appreciation of her strong character.

Today, Rivera's dream has come true. The Parque Ecológico Bosque de Cinquera is widely promoted on ecotourism and mainstream travel sites. It covers more than 5,000 hectares, or more than 12,000 acres. The trees are protected from logging, which had started in earnest after the war to provide income for the impoverished village.

As a result of Rivera's work, there is a new El Salvador in Cinquera, displaying the spectacular beauty of the forest and creeks. But Cinquera has not papered over the war or left it behind. It stands silently in a bombed-out church. On the façade, mural portraits of Archbishop Romero and the town's murdered Catholic priest announce the price of freedom in Cinquera.

Don't Get In That Ambulance

I first met Brad Kazmerzak when he was bartending at Soho, a classy bar and nightclub tucked away in a Spanish-style courtyard in Santa Barbara. It was conveniently located next to my publisher's office and opened at 5 p.m.

Brad was a perfect bartender—friendly, open, and with a quick laugh. He made good money at the job, but he felt trapped. On the side, he was a photographer in a beautiful natural environment filled with nature photographers.

It did not take much to convince him to come to El Salvador with me in 2002. I'd already told him my war stories over draft beers. Now, I pointed out, he would have a whole new canvas to make his art. We would travel to all parts of the countryside and we would continue my search for Gilberto. Plus, we'd be helping in the here and now, which appealed to Brad's charitable side. We both would carry big bags of medicine from Direct Relief International (DRI) to deliver to a people's clinic in one of the poorest and most gang-infested parts of San Salvador: La Chacra.

Since its founding in 1948, Direct Relief International (now Direct Relief), a Santa Barbara–based nonprofit medical relief organization, has quickly became one of a few major players in international health by funneling massive donations of drugs and medical equipment from major U.S. and foreign companies into more than 90 countries. Their secret is to keep a small administrative staff in Santa Barbara and then rely on volunteers like me and Brad to visit their recipients around the world and report back on our findings. I had heard about their good work and was particularly impressed by their CEO, a former Peace Corps administrator, Thomas Tighe. I had started volunteering for them and was ready to make more deliveries of medical equipment and antibiotics.

Brad was tasked with transporting a 50-pound bag of medicine, and I had a 30-pound bag. He would go out a day early and head out to a small village near the Honduran border to shoot a dental and medical clinic. He would photograph eye operations as well as bloody tooth extractions. It was a long way from spectacular photos of Pacific Ocean waves crashing against the cliffs of California. But he went with a lot of excitement, if a little apprehension.

Since he was going out solo a day ahead of me, I gave him two simple instructions: Don't talk to anybody on the plane, and only take a taxi cab with a symbol on the door indicating it was radio-dispatched. I had been told that taxis with radios could quickly call their dispatch if there was any trouble.

But Brad's mellow, engaging personality got the best of him. On the plane, he sat next to a man whose family controlled a coffee plantation, a designer coffee brand, and a string of coffee bars, something new and exciting in a country known for exporting its highest-quality beans and serving its low-quality coffee locally. When the man offered Brad a ride to his hotel, he couldn't refuse.

Shortly thereafter, on the main highway from the airport to the city, the coffee grower ran into the back of a military patrol jeep. Nobody was hurt, but this is not the way to introduce yourself to the local gendarmes. Eventually, shouting turned into joking, and all was well. The driver was, after all, a plantation owner, with a gringo in the car. When Brad told me what happened, I couldn't help thinking that if he and his new acquaintance had run into the back of an army vehicle in 1981, the interaction may well have ended in death and disappearance.

I arrived the next day, to deliver medical supplies and continue my search for information about Gilberto. A few days later, as Brad and I were walking from our hotel to a grocery store, we passed through a clearly upper-middle-class neighborhood.

Parked in front of one of the houses was a stripped-down former ambulance parked against the curb with several young men hanging around it.

It was instantly clear to me that this was not a regular ambulance, and that the loitering young men were not first responders. I also knew that, as in many Latin American countries, kidnapping for ransom in El Salvador is a thriving business, particularly among gangs. Usually the victim is returned, but many times they are never seen again. So as we approached, I whispered to Brad not to talk and not to slow down.

He was a very fit, big guy, and I was a not-as-fit medium guy, and as we approached, a big woman filled in behind us. "We are an ambulance and out of gas," a young man explained. As we passed by and looked in, all the ambulance had inside it was two chairs—not very convincing.

We did not slow. We did not speak. We watched as the men seemed to make a mental calculation of whether it would be worth putting their three against us two. Nothing ended up happening, and I was glad Brad was with me.

In 2006, I cajoled my son George IV into spending two weeks in San Salvador, studying Spanish in a CIS immersion program and living with a host family. He was 20, had been in a Spanish immersion class for several years, and, if not eager, was at least curious about this place his father seemed obsessed with. I was going to leave him for two weeks, then come back to pick him up. Just before I left him, we were walking near the University of El Salvador campus, taking a shortcut I thought I had discovered. Our route took us down a busy street with car body shops spewing smoke and wielding cutting torches like a scene from hell. As we passed them, we felt conspicuously foreign, as though the men in the garages were sizing us up. A car began following us in the street. A tattooed young man leaned out the passenger side and said, "Where are you going?" We didn't respond, kept walking, went faster, adopting the body language of people heading somewhere important. The car continued to tail us, the man in the passenger seat glaring at these two white guys in the wrong neighborhood. The car finally drove off. To this day, my son gives me grief when I say I know a quick way to get somewhere. It gives me some comfort to know that he knows to avoid being in the wrong place at the wrong time—and, of course, that we did not end up gagged and bound in the back seat of that menacing car.

It was a tough time for him, being a shy guy amid strangers conversing in another language and eating unfamiliar foods. When he first returned, he did not talk about a glamorous adventure. But as years have gone by, he's made clear that it enriched his sense of what the world contains, its good and its bad. I admire his courage in taking the plunge and wonder if at 20 I would have been willing to indulge my father's whim.

There were dangers in El Salvador during the war and dangers after the war. The deportation of thousands of gang members from Southern California back to El Salvador during and after the war worsened the crime situation in many San Salvador neighborhoods. These young men came back to a country they often had no connection to. The gangs offered community, respect, and money. We were witnessing the aftermath of a really bad time. Only later would a Salvadoran president try to fix this problem with tactics used throughout Salvadoran history: round people up, including the innocents, lock them up, and throw away the key.

La Chacra

On my 2001 trip to El Salvador, carrying a huge and heavy load of used dental equipment for Maria Madre Clinic in La Chacra, clinic supporters in the U.S. recommended I use Luis Alfredo Alvarado as my driver. I was assured he was trustworthy and able to navigate not just the roads, but also the gangs and police.

When he showed up at the airport, I was a bit taken aback. He had a bushy beard, wore a red beret, and kept a photo of Che Guevara and Fidel Castro on the dashboard of his battered cab. He looked like Che himself, and that's how he introduced himself—as Che—and what I continued to call him as he ferried my traveling companions and me across El Salvador over the coming years. Also perched on the dashboard was a half-smoked cigar. As we made the drive in from the airport, Che filled me in on the latest drama in Cuba. Castro was alleging that an American who had lived in El Salvador had plotted to assassinate him. Che was upset and angry.

Luis—or rather, Che—was a former FMLN fighter. When he invited me to his home for dinner one night, he showed me his grenade launcher, pointing it at me with a big grin. His taxi often seemed close to disintegrating. Potholes would send it (and us) shuddering, and the back wheel well, which Che would occasionally adjust, was attached to the car body with bonding glue. The car felt dicey, but Che drove slowly and methodically —never exceeding 30 miles an hour, and taking the cab out of gear on downhill sections to save gas. He never got lost.

Everywhere we went, people knew Che. Many of his fellow guerrillas were now working for the government, or in other official positions. In La Chacra, one of San Salvador's most marginal communities on what has come to be known as the *cinturón miseria*, or "belt of misery," around the capital, Che navigated the winding, hilly streets deftly, but he also curtly acknowledged the gang members on the street corners. Almost half the residents of La Chacra are unemployed. Many are underemployed street vendors who make as little as $100 a month. The neighborhood divides the turf of one Central America's most notorious gangs, or *maras*, Salvatrucha 13, from its rival, the 18th Street gang.

Over my years of working with DRI, I "adopted" the Maria Madre de los Pobres clinic in La Chacra, always hiring Che to negotiate the neighborhood so I could bring the clinic bags of medicines and other supplies I'd brought from the States. I was glad to support DRI's work, which had become part of my own mission to make restitution to El Salvador. But it was clear that the payments had to be bigger, and that the overall debt Americans, including myself, owed was much greater than we could ever meet on our own.

On a 2005 trip, I went there with Bill Morton-Smith, Direct Relief International's Chief Medical Officer. It was Bill's first stop on an intense three-country swing through El Salvador, Guatemala, and Honduras, checking on the capacity and effectiveness of almost a dozen different clinics and hospitals that hoped to become partners of DRI.

Che told us he would take us on the safe route to La Chacra. Bill had related that on his last trip to the clinic, as Che had driven down the windy street through the outskirts of the capital, they had passed a woman savagely beating a man with a rock. Che did not stop—he did not even slow down. He knew it was a time and place that visitors would not be welcome, and that nothing good would come from stopping.

Bill and DRI tried to focus on what they could help with: bringing medicine the locals could not afford, scrounging used medical equipment in the U.S., and setting up multinational aid teams of doctors willing to donate their skills to rural residents. In La Chacra, that meant treating patients with intense cases of worms—a Third World issue around which best practices are not always clear. If you quickly treat patients at the first sign of worms, they may simply re-ingest the water and dirt that infected them in the first place. Bill would argue that it is a much more efficient use of scarce antiparasitic medicines to wait for the body to be wracked with parasites, and then administer a major dose.

The bacterial brew in La Chacra is worsened by noxious air pollution as well as the pollution in the Acelhuate River, which runs through La Chacra and has been described as El Salvador's most polluted river. Stacks of trash sit on its many little islands. Rather than gurgling, the water foams. But neighborhood residents, whose wood and brick huts cover steep slopes above the river, bathe and swim and play in its muck. They drink from even more polluted sources. Upper respiratory problems, intestinal parasites, and other disorders are endemic, as well as the scourge of poor countries: diabetes and heart disease.

Set against this backdrop, the Maria Madre de los Pobres (Mary Mother of the Poor) compound is like an oasis. Inside high fences are a clinic, school, senior food center, and a simple but elegant church at the top of a steep hill. When we arrived there in 2005, Che helped us with introductions, then retired to the shade as we toured the medical facilities.

I was happy to see that, in the dental clinic, tools I'd brought three years earlier were being used to help a patient. But it was shocking to learn that, unlike on previous visits, there were no antibiotics at all in the pharmacy. The shelves were bare. It was to be a grim refrain that Bill would hear throughout his trip.

Clinics in the Global South like Maria Madre desperately seek amoxicillin, the workhorse of the worldwide war on infection and disease. Because it is in such demand throughout the world, drug companies do not like to donate it to DRI or other relief organizations. They would be undercutting their own profitable product pipelines. So they donate more potent but less familiar antibiotics like Lorabid. I had brought a duffel bag with 30 pounds of Lorabid to deliver, and while I was glad to do so, it was obvious that this wouldn't go far enough to meet the considerable need. DRI and Third World clinics often go out and buy amoxicillin on their own just to have it on hand, but this did not seem to have been an option for Maria Madre at the time.

While Maria Madre has U.S. sponsors who include pharmacists and physicians, many clinics don't. They hand out whatever antibiotic they have on the shelf, and it is notoriously difficult to monitor patients who take the medication. One of Maria Madre's assets is U.S. pharmacologist Mary Frances

Ross, who has a Ph.D. in pharmacology and is a professor at Ferris State University in Michigan. She has gathered medicine in her religious community in Kalamazoo and provided ongoing medical advice to the clinic. She and others are concerned with the use of antibiotics throughout El Salvador. If clinics treating the poor don't have amoxicillin, they prescribe more powerful donated antibiotics. The result is that powerful antibiotics are going up against powerful bugs, and sometimes the bugs get a powerful boost of resistance. For example, if a chronically ill patient gets enough of an antibiotic to beat back, but not kill, an infection, that particular bug can develop immunities to that drug. Patients may stop taking drugs before treatment is done because they run out of money, or because the clinics treating them run out of the drug to give them. "The bugs in La Chacra," Bill explained, "are going to get resistant to Lorabid because that's what they are going to use here."

Around a picnic table outside the residential part of Maria Madre, Father Daniel Sanchez, who built this amazing mission, explained just how bad the situation in La Chacra had become. Sanchez was born in Spain and came to El Salvador in the late 1970s. In the 1980s, he was forced to flee La Chacra when it became a dangerous battlefield between guerrillas with the FMLN and the government. The neighborhood was bombed several times by U.S.-supplied Salvadoran Air Force jets. Like many priests who worked in poor neighborhoods or campos, Sanchez was viewed by the government as an enemy. He fled to the mountains when the death squads threatened him. Today, he explained, at least 4,000 people come from 18 surrounding neighborhoods to use the clinic, even though it is in the middle of a gang-infested area.

It is not the gangs, though, that most worry Father Sanchez. It is the economy. "The situation is the worst now," he told us over drinks of freshly squeezed orange juice. "The economy is going down, and the poverty is going up."

The government and the people, he said, "are jittery." Riots in neighboring Nicaragua—Che had told us with a mischievous grin that he had just returned from Managua—had erupted over high gasoline prices and plans to raise bus fares.

"What happened in Nicaragua could happen here," Sanchez explained. It was another message we heard often on this trip. While economies in much of Latin America had been growing over the past decade, the number of people living in poverty had not budged. Instead, the wealthy had accrued more power, as manufacturers opened cheap textile and electronics plants and foreign investment climbed.

At the same time, food prices were up. Many countries, under pressure from the U.S., had dropped subsidies for their basic food products, and thus prices of tortillas, beans, and vegetable oils had climbed during the 2000s. So had fuel prices. This had a massive toll on marginal workers, who often relied on public transportation.

Before and after its involvement in the Salvadoran Civil War, the U.S. preached a liturgy of free trade and open markets. But it was clear that free trade meant U.S. companies could move their factories and plants to low-wage nations, like El Salvador. It meant food subsidies by Latin governments were frowned upon and U.S. corn, flour, and oil exports devastated subsistence farmers and small landowners. The huge inequalities that dated in El Salvador back to the turn of the nineteenth century still existed. The Spanish exploited and killed the indigenous populations, and their heirs pushed peasants off their lands to grow indigo, and then coffee, and now to produce textiles. Bill and I were trying to counter the ravages of the open markets. We could only do so much.

War Machines

During that same 2005 trip to El Salvador, my path crossed with that of newly appointed Secretary of State Condoleezza Rice. She was an archconservative and a Bush loyalist, replacing the more pragmatic world diplomat Colin Powell. Her four-country barnstorming tour of Latin America would also include Brazil, the region's largest and most economically important country; Chile, the second most important economic engine of the region; and Colombia, recipient of the second largest dose of American military aid in the world because of both its fight against guerrillas and the birth of the cocaine cartels.

When the State Department jet landed at the airport, the reason for Rice's visit became apparent. There to greet her were representatives of the small contingent of soldiers El Salvador had sent to Iraq as a symbolic gesture of endorsement for the Bush invasion. Her stop was to be a pointed thank-you to the only Latin American country that had provided token support to the Bush Administration. Rice also wanted to make sure her thanks would help prop up the presidency of local tycoon Tony Saca, a conservative from the ARENA party, which during the war had deep ties to the death squads. Saca, who was president from 2004 to 2009, was later convicted by Salvadoran courts of embezzling some $260 million from the government. He was sentenced to 10 years in prison.

From the moment I had heard Rice was coming to El Salvador, I had wanted to personally cover her visit. It was not just that this was momentous for El Salvador; it was a chance to cover an individual who will go down in history as a critical architect of the Bush legacy. Plus, how often does a reporter from Woodland and later Chico get to cover a Secretary of State? I would get to see the big boys and girls of journalism working their trade in a far-off land.

And, I thought, it might be a kind of déjà vu. It would be one more trip to the drugstore of journalistic jags, adrenaline rushes, and tight deadlines. And it would be a chance to acquaint, or perhaps reacquaint, myself with the Salvadoran press corps.

Within hours of my arrival in San Salvador, I was on the phone with the U.S. Embassy, trying to determine how credentialing would work and what Rice's itinerary would be. I figured I would encounter a huge security operation with hurdles, checkpoints, and large spaces between the press and the Secretary.

I was pleasantly surprised. The press office was cordial and responsive. There was only one handoff, and after several phone calls, I was told that I needed to get credentials from the Salvadoran government, but that if I showed up at the Casa Presidencial, the Salvadoran White House, on the evening of Rice's arrival, I could probably cover her joint press briefing with President Saca.

With a Santa Barbara Police Department press badge—dated but authentic-looking—and a Salvadoran government press credential issued in 2003 for the last presidential election, I climbed into a cab and headed for the Casa. I had expected heavy security, assuming that the government would fear anti-U.S. demonstrations, especially after the rumbles in Nicaragua the week before. I was wrong.

The cab dropped me in front of one of several gates to the Casa, and I walked to a nearby guardhouse. I told the lone guard at the guardhouse my mission, and he made a few calls. There was no press in sight. No lurking soldiers. Nothing. The calm was broken by a trio from the nearby Radisson Hotel who were carrying extra gold-trim plates that displayed the official seal of El Salvador and needed to be rushed in before the state dinner with Rice. I wondered if somebody had been invited at the last minute—someone's in-laws, I amused myself imagining, though I knew bankers would be much likelier additions.

Finally, the guard gave me instructions to walk all the way around the presidential compound to the back gate, the one facing the Guzman Museum, where that night a rock concert was in full swing. Passing only one lonely soldier on patrol, I hiked to the back entrance just in time to see a gaggle of what in any country in the world would be quickly identified as a "press pack." Guys with badges and camera bags slung around their necks, gals clutching notebooks and tape recorders, everybody under the age of 30.

I quickly joined the pack, walked through the back gate of the Presidential House, and with the others obediently dropped my camera bag in a pile and stepped back. A Salvadoran soldier with a dog approached the pile, but the dog seemed even less interested than the soldier. There were smirks among the press and a few comments about whose bag the dog would smell first. The bomb sniff was done in less than a minute, and we all walked up the driveway to the press entrance of the auditorium where the joint press conference was to be held.

A representative from the U.S. Embassy walked up and introduced herself to me. They'd known I was coming, she said. I figured this was low-key security. Everybody knew everybody else in the Salvadoran press corps—there weren't more than 25 journalists in all—but I was the stranger, funky badges and all.

Inside, I was reminded that press coverage of big events in small countries is no different than press coverage of little events in big countries. Seating is critical. Velvet ropes separate the washed from the unwashed. The TV camera is king.

I was directed to the "foreign in-country press" area, a small roped compound where I was the sole prisoner, well away from the lecterns and without a seat. We were about to begin the worldwide press ritual of "hurry up and wait" when there was a sudden chow call from the back.

We all streamed out into a small courtyard, where the presidential staff had set up a press food table of bite-sized sandwiches, soft drinks, and cookies. Salvadoran press is no different than American: Free food is one of the few job benefits, and it is taken where it can be gotten. The bite-sized sandwiches disappeared and were replaced with huge pans of French-fried potato cubes. Only this seemed to slow the feeding frenzy.

While wolfing down a couple of sandwiches, I encountered the enigmatic Ernie Palumbo. I had met him on one of my first trips back to El Salvador, when he was introduced to me as a person who had been in the country for a long time and knew everybody and their business. At the time, he was working for a major U.S. apparel company, helping to monitor working conditions in order that this blue-chip brand name not be smeared by allegations that it was using children in sweatshop conditions or paying horrible wages to produce its high-end products.

A few days previously, over greasy Chinese food at one of his favorite restaurants, Palumbo had given me nothing about himself or what he was doing. Like many expats, he was suspicious of parachute journalists and wary of sharing information with somebody whom he did not know or have a clue of their true motives. Now, however, inside the velvet rope, we quickly fell into conversation. He told me that he no longer worked for the textile industry and instead was stringing for several major news organizations. Business, he admitted, was slow.

It wouldn't help that Rice would bring with her at least 10 traveling press corps members from the biggest names in U.S. media. It was this contingent that provided the first notion that style does reign over substance when you are manufacturing the news. There would not be big scoops here. The news would be manufactured by the State Department press office and obediently rewritten by these reporters from the biggest news outlets in the U.S. They had to be there, but this was nowhere when it came to breaking news or better explaining why U.S. policies were not addressing Latin America's biggest issue:

the huge gap between rich and poor and the inability of U.S. global solutions to address global poverty.

As we streamed back into the conference room and continued to wait for Rice and Saca to appear, an animated debate broke out between a stern, matronly representative of the U.S. Embassy and a young, not-to-be-pushed Salvadoran protocol functionary. It seemed that the seats up front had been nonchalantly taken by the U.S. press contingent who traveled with Rice: This was their show, and if they were going to be spoonfed, they didn't want to be far from the spoon. But these seats were also understood to be reserved for big shots from the U.S. Embassy. The Salvadoran functionary was furious that her friends from the Embassy would have to sit at the back, but in this case, *The New York Times* and *The Washington Post* trumped the colonels.

We had been told to be at the Casa at 6:30 for a prompt 7:30 press conference. At 8, we seemed to be rolling: A Salvadoran press officer got up to the microphone and explained the rules for this pony show. Only three questions from the Salvadoran press would be allowed, one each for TV, radio, and print. The North American press would also get three questions. It seemed pretty clear that my one question, which I had been planning all day, was not going to be among them. Not my first dismount at a big rodeo.

Almost an hour later, we hadn't gotten started, but a clownish Salvadoran press officer coating the lectern area with bug spray gave the press something to laugh about. At first, I assumed this was a precaution against mosquito-borne dengue fever, but later I realized it was probably just to make sure there wouldn't be any bugs flying around Rice's head as she delivered her sound bites for TV.

Finally, at almost 9 p.m., there was a bustle outside. On the long driveway, a caravan of dark-windowed SUVs pulled up, followed by an ambulance with its lights flashing. Rice had finally arrived.

We waited another 20 minutes as she met privately with Saca. People entered the side door in proper protocols from both countries. The grand entrance was achieved with much flair and formality, with Saca and Rice standing before carefully placed flags of their two countries.

Rice seemed tired and, perhaps unsurprisingly, had little of real content to say. She called this a "really just wonderful reception." And she praised El Salvador as "one of our strongest allies in the hemisphere, an ally that we admire as a strong fighter in the global war on terrorism and a country that, having known terrorism itself, is willing to stand up and fight it." This struck me as a brazen rewriting of Salvadoran history. The terrorists had been the death squads, the Matanza of Maximilian, but she seemed to be referring to the guerrillas and the FMLN. Now, the American war machine had turned its attention to Iraq. El Salvador was just a quick stop for one of the most powerful American functionaries.

The State Department press corps asked about free trade and, with what struck me as a surprising zinger, whether the U.S. would drop its protection of the sugar industry and other agricultural industries (like avocados and citrus) that are protected against Latin American farm exports. Rice gave a non-answer, neither saying she supported her own country's high barriers to trade nor saying she would work to overturn them. The U.S. would "give up" these subsidies only when the World Trade Organization ordered it to, she said. This is the free trade the Bush Administration preached. No wonder our Latin American neighbors cry "foul."

The Salvadoran press asked a couple of soft questions, closing with one about whether El Salvador would receive more military aid from the U.S. Rice responded that the U.S. had a "long-standing program" of military support for El Salvador and that the Bush Administration planned to militarily help those countries that helped the U.S. in Iraq and Afghanistan. In other words, there would be a military payoff for El Salvador for its token support in Iraq.

Alone behind my rope, I felt both comfortable and more or less invisible. I had wanted to ask Rice why—after a decade of U.S. preaching in the 1990s that foreign investment, low trade barriers, and the conversion of Latin economies from commodities production to cheap manufacturing—poverty in Latin America remained so high. Surely she knew that poverty was at the root of revolutions in the '70s and '80s from Colombia to Peru to El Salvador. Didn't she think, I imagined myself asking, that it was time for another plan, another idea, a new paradigm?

But I think I know how she would have answered: She'd say that the fight against terrorism around the world was now the most important American interest, and that free trade should be given another decade to work, and even that while we had mostly forgotten Latin America since 9/11, it was important to America's future.

As she slipped out for a state dinner on that gold-plated seal of El Salvador, I slipped back outside. I headed back to the hotel and a dinner at El Pueblo Viejo, a favorite of locals for its loud atmosphere and family-friendly staff. I had lots of colorful notes about the press, but really only vacuous statements from Rice. Her appearance was a stage act, part of the projection of U.S. power and influence around the world.

Guatemala

The next day, Bill and I took a quick 45-minute flight from San Salvador to Guatemala City. On a previous trip, I had taken the six-hour bus ride between the two capitals, but there were increasing reports of bandits on the Guatemalan side. Bill had a lot of territory to cover, and we had less time to risk on adventure this year. I was happy to be safe.

We were met at the airport by Idahoan Craig Sinkinson, a former emergency room physician.

Our transport was a minivan, crammed to the ceiling with medical examination-room stools. Our destination was one of the most beautiful spots in Central America, Lake Atitlán, high in the mountains of Guatemala. Bill's job was to determine whether Sinkinson's brand-new clinic and a hospital on the other side of Atitlán were ready for major shipments of medical supplies from DRI. My mission was to see Atitlán, a place that in the early '80s was dangerous enough that I decided not to enter it. In the 1980s, the government was in a full-fledged war against leftist guerrillas and indigenous populations. As in El Salvador, journalists were not safe even with their TV signs taped to their van windows for their forays into the countryside.

On the two-hour drive from gritty Guatemala City to the picturesque Lake Atitlán, Sinkinson explained how he had given up practicing medicine in Southern California and moved to Santa Cruz la Laguna, a community of 900 Kaqchikel people perched on a steep mountain along the lake.

"It has always been my passion to go somewhere and provide medical care where there was no medical care," he explained. He was introduced to the culture of international philanthropy in the 1970s, when he accompanied medical relief teams into Mexico. In 2002, Sinkinson decided to write a book on Spanish medical terminology. No such book existed, and it was meant to provide not only useful clinical information but also a means to help train young medical workers in Spanish-speaking countries. In the process, he sat on a panel on medical translations at a major medical convention in Guatemala and met a Guatemalan doctor. They took a day off from the convention to look at rural medical clinics, and when they toured Atitlán, something clicked for him.

There were no medical clinics on the lake, though at least 20,000 to 30,000 Guatemalans live around it. There is a nearby hospital, but it takes well over an hour to get to and has limited facilities.

After the van pulled up to the lakefront, we quickly loaded the clinic examination stools and bags into a 20-foot skiff with an impatient skipper and a rather small motor. In minutes, we were off to Santa Cruz, which is only accessible by boat. About 20 minutes later, we pulled up to a spectacularly beautiful and rugged mountainside where a small village clung to ledges and clearings. A ragtag group of boys, who looked no older than seven or eight, began running along the short waterfront and down the tiny dock to meet us. These were Sinkinson's "muchachos," ready, for a few quetzales, to haul luggage and equipment up a tremendously steep road to the village above. Later I learned that they were actually 10 to 12 years old, but that years of poor nutrition had taken a toll on their growth.

Sinkinson's clinic was in the town square, in a relatively new building that faces the village school, the Catholic Church, and the town offices. The complex was built by the previous mayor, who agreed to allow Sinkinson to move the clinic into the bottom floor but insisted on keeping the top floor as his personal penthouse. The mayor didn't last long, and Sinkinson now has clinic offices on both floors. The new town mayor, like the old one, is not from the community and has little interest in the medical needs of the Kaqchikel of Santa Cruz.

The challenges are daunting. Malnutrition is the number-one health problem in this region. But malnutrition is an economic issue, based in the poverty of the population. Sinkinson has decided his clinic will focus on an easier but also devastating health issue: high maternal and infant mortality rates.

While the U.S. has a maternal death rate of two per one million population—a relatively high number compared with other advanced Western nations—Guatemala has a maternal death rate of 500 per one million population. That is the highest in Central America. (In a telling contrast to the difference in culture and urbanization, the much smaller and more urbanized El Salvador has maternal death rates even lower than the U.S., according to the World Health Organization.) Near Lake Atitlán, babies are routinely delivered by *comadronas*, midwives, who tend to use no gloves, let alone sterilized equipment. The maternal death rate around Lake Atitlán is even higher than the rest of the country.

Only a few weeks before we'd arrived, Sinkinson related, a 16-year-old Santa Cruz mother had died in childbirth in the middle of Semana Santa, the Holy Week. She had bled to death.

The family of the expectant mother tends to pay one rate for the delivery of a male—say, 50 quetzals—and half that rate if the baby is a female. If there is a problem, a miscarriage or a death at birth, comadronas are paid much less. If complications develop, the hospital is far enough away not to seem like a viable option: If a boat can be found swiftly, it can take up to an hour to travel to the main village of Panajachel, and then—assuming an ambulance has been dispatched from the hospital—over another hour to drive to the hospital. Sinkinson explained that he hoped to provide care closer to home, and that, to build trust and relationships with the locals, he hoped to pay comadronas to bring expectant mothers to his clinic for delivery. Such a system would rely on Guatemalan tradition while providing a safety net for emergencies.

The next day, Bill and I were sped by boat across Atitlán to an even grander endeavor. The spectacular views of the three Atitlán volcanoes, San Pedro, Tolimán and Atitlán, were obscured by the haze characteristic of the start of the rainy season. Lake Atitlán was formed tens of thousands of years ago with a mega-eruption of a single volcano. Over thousands of years, the cauldron filled with water, creating what many believe is one of the most beautiful lakes in the world.

On the far shore, in the bustling small city of Santiago, we were picked up by three-wheeled tuk-tuks that took us several miles to the far outskirts of town, to the remnants of what was once the town hospital.

In 1990, a group of Santiagans had marched to the military garrison next door to the hospital to protest the treatment of indigenous peoples by army forces. It was the tail end of the ferocious, genocidal epoch when indigenous people were massacred as the army fought a guerrilla movement to a bloody standoff. There are contradictory accounts of what happened that day in 1990, but 14 Santiagans were killed and 21 wounded by army soldiers. Afterward, the local indigenous residents refused to pass by the army garrison at all, and the hospital eventually closed. By the early 2000s, it was a flop house for homeless drug users and bored youth. Its walls were falling in, its floors covered with human excrement.

Today, a monument to the courage of the 14 who were massacred is just around the corner from the hospital, which—with the help of a handful of international doctors and community organizers—was reopening. A team of American, Dutch, and Mexican doctors was staffing what was then a clinic, and would soon be a hospital, around the clock. They were offering health care for free. Small amounts of money came in via contributions from Americans, and locals were helping put the word out.

The facilities were immaculate, but when we entered the operating room, we found the bane of so many health facilities across the Global South that depend upon foreign generosity: expensive and elaborate equipment that is not fully functional, because minor parts—not available locally—have worn out, or because something has broken and no one locally knows how to fix it.

A few minutes later, we met Robert, a ponytailed Southerner who looked to be in his late fifties. He was toiling in a make-shift woodworking shop, making exquisite wooden shelves and cabinets to be used throughout the hospital. Back in the U.S., he told us, he does custom woodworking for Walmart. In his time off, he comes to Santiago, building a hospital for no pay and no recognition.

Perhaps he has his own reparations to make. I didn't ask. I was struck by the fact that in the farthest parts of this world, there are people from other countries and cultures giving their skill and precious time to improve the lives of those less fortunate. This reflects a spirit reassuringly at odds with those who plan our battles and wars.

Memorial

When I finally left Guatemala in 2005, I was both thrilled and depressed. I had a new story to tell of Americans who were trying to fix the damage of decades of civil war and American-backed brutality in Central America. But while it felt good to help Bill in his rounds, I was no closer to taking care of my real business: finding Gilberto Moran's grave, finding his family.

So, on my last day in El Salvador, I tried again. I hired Che for the day, and our first stop was to visit El Salvador's newest war memorial, in the main central park of San Salvador, Cuscatlán. Clearly influenced by Maya Lin's design for the Vietnam War memorial in Washington, D.C., the Monument to Memory and Truth is made up of a series of black granite panels filled with the names of more than 25,000 civilians. All are known to have been killed or disappeared by the government and its allies in the death squads between 1980 and 1994.

The names appear in chronological order by date of death, and the longest lists are from 1981 and 1982. I looked for Gilberto's name and couldn't find it. He was murdered, I tell myself, but he is not remembered on this wall. It was as though he had disappeared.

I was surprised that on two different visits to the memorial, I saw very few other visitors. Perhaps Salvadorans do not want to revisit this part of their history, no matter what side they took during the war. On the other hand, it is a stark reminder of the incalculable cost of the civil war.

My disappointment at not finding Gilberto's name grew as Che drove us to Soyapango. We went up the hill on the road overlooking the Agua Caliente power plant, to the place where, as best I could reconstruct it, Gilberto, Joaquin Zuniga, and I had been shot. It was the first time I'd been back, and I doubt I will ever want to return.

Dug-out positions on the crest of the hill gave a panoramic view of the road leading to the power plant. I can imagine that this is where the Treasury Police sat and watched us slowly walk down the road, and where they had a clear view of the journalists directly below them.

The scene of the shooting, from the vantage point of the Treasury Police.
Photo by George Thurlow.

Che picked up a long stick and mimicked a soldier shooting down into the roadway. It was funny and not so funny. Maybe this wasn't exactly the spot they shot from, but I could feel bad karma rising from the ground.

The shopkeeper of a soda stand nearby told us that she had been in the neighborhood since 1980 and remembered all the fighting. But not here, she said. Elsewhere. She did not remember the attack on the power station.

Not soon enough, we left Agua Caliente and headed to the public records office for the city of San Salvador. Several people had told us we should go there to look for Gilberto's death certificate, which would tell us where he was buried, and maybe even where he was born.

The *alcaldía*, or central government office, is a complex of Spanish Colonial–style buildings in an industrial area of San

Driver Luis "Che" Alvarado stands where Treasury Police were stationed when they opened fire on journalists on the street below.

Salvador, and it feels like its hallways have been full of bu-
reaucrats for centuries. Che said that one of his old FMLN
comrades was now working in the media office at city hall, so
we headed there first, but the friend was out. When we asked
a bored office functionary about our quest, he just shrugged.
Strangers looking for death certificates was clearly not something he wanted to get into.

We walked to the far side of the complex, where Che assumed
the attitude of an insider, heading straight into an office and
immediately asking to see the "jefe." We were quickly told that
the jefe was out and nobody knew when he would back. "How
about the subjefe?" Che asked.

A diligent-looking young bureaucrat emerged from around a
corner and asked us our business. He made no effort to invite
us into his office, so Che, somewhat irritated, asked to go there
himself. The office turned out to be nothing more than a desk
behind a room divider.

Che related our request: Could we look at death records from
April 1981 for San Salvador? The bureaucrat, who seemed
both stubborn and irked by Che's attitude, responded that he
would not help us. But Che did not back down, and finally, the
man relented, asking an assistant to pull out a book from 1981.

My excitement grew. The death records of the era are contained
in ledger books, not unlike those found in the local cemeteries,
carrying dates on their spines and listing, inside, the names of
the deceased and the circumstances of their deaths. I stood to
look over the assistant's shoulder as she turned to April. One
man, I see, died as a result of a *bomba*, or bomb.

After a few minutes of turning the pages back into March and forward into May, she turned and said that there was nothing about a Gilberto Moran killed in Soyapango. We would need to go to the Soyapango alcaldía or maybe even the one nearer to Agua Caliente, they said. There was nothing here.

Another fruitless search. Another dead end.

As we were walking out of the office and into the courtyard, Che greeted an older woman. They did not know each other well, but Che confirmed they were both in the FMLN, and now he asked her for help. She suggested that maybe Gilberto was born in San Salvador, and therefore would have a birth record. But what, she asks, is his birthdate?

That's easy, I responded: Same day as mine, November 10, 1951.

She was gone in an instant and didn't return for some time. When she did, the news was the same: No records. No Gilberto Moran.

As a reporter in the U.S., I'd learned, you make some clever moves to find the important documents, and then you write your story. In El Salvador, that search proceeds very differently. Records are not well-kept. There are huge gaps in documents. And government employees can be suspicious of people dredging up the past, particularly when it involves somebody shot by the military. In particular, having a clearly FMLN veteran stirring the pot did not quicken the responses. In retrospect, it is very possible that there were records for Gilberto. We may have been the wrong people to ask for them.

Also, maybe it feels simpler to keep things buried, try to move forward, not get involved in a gringo's uncomfortable and potentially troublesome quest, and forget the horrors neighbors wrought on neighbors.

Nuns Who Led the Way

In 2023, I returned to the Maria Madre clinic with DRI face masks and vitamins for pregnant women. In the pharmacy, waiting for the influx of patients from the La Chacra neighborhood, was Sister Patti Rogulki. We chatted briefly, and then I was pulled away to watch the students from the Maria Madre school march to their chapel, all carrying portraits of the martyred Archbishop Romero.

The next day, there was a bigger march, starting at the Chapel at Divina Providencia Hospital, where Romero had been shot by right-wing death-squad members while leading a mass. Some 300 people were there, mostly older, but with a sprinkling of youth. Many held signs, and even more held photos of Romero. An impromptu souvenir stand had sprung up at the entrance to the church, selling Romero T-shirts. I bought a safari hat, having forgotten how merciless the Salvadoran sun can be. It cost two dollars.

As the march began, I spotted Sister Patti, and we walked and talked together. In her eighties, she was as full of life and spirit as any teenager walking in a small-town homecoming parade. The march wound through some residential neighborhoods and ended at the downtown cathedral.

She told me that she had been influenced to become a nun by her aunt, who was one too. Sister Patti said she had first joined the Felician Sisters, an order founded in the 1850s in Poland with almost 700 members in North America today. But she found the Felicians' mission a little stifling. It emphasized teaching and education, and Patti wanted to be out working with the poor and marginalized. "I wanted to work with people," she said, waving her multicolored umbrella like it was a shepherd's staff. She left the Felicians and joined the Sisters for Christian Community, a non-aligned, self-supporting organization of nuns focused on working with the most destitute populations. It has no "mother home," and its sisters work around the world.

In the late '70s and early '80s, the "liberation theology" movement was catching on among progressive Catholics in the First and Third worlds. Liberation theology argued that Jesus worked with the poor, championed the poor, and ministered first to them, and that the Catholic Church should follow the same mission. Liberation theology became especially influential in Latin America, and it was a powerful ideology among many priests in El Salvador. It was one reason the military and security forces were so suspicious, and at times murderous, toward Catholic priests and nuns. After all, helping the poor was viewed as helping the guerrillas.

Sister Patti believed that contemporary Catholic doctrines called on nuns to leave their safety nets and go out in the community. "That is what I wanted. We were called to work with people, not for people." In 1989, she said, she came to El Salvador and "just fell in love with the people." She is not sure when or if she will ever leave. She teaches art classes for both the clinic students and for members of the community. She started with a drawing of a clown, and now everybody in La Chacra draws clowns. Clowns are an important cultural icon in Latin America and in El Salvador, fusing indigenous characters with modern-day entertainers. El Salvador even has a National Clown Day.

The marching route took us by Salvadoran icon the Monument to the Divine Savior of the World, a 59-foot statue of Jesus Christ standing on top of the world globe and pointing a finger to heaven. It was built in 1942 atop the tomb of Salvadoran President Manuel Araujo.

I have enormous respect for Catholics like Sister Patti who, driven by faith, seek to remedy the ravages of poverty and oppression. And yet I can't help but think that this giant sculpture also reflects the history of Spanish conquest—driven, as they were, by God, Glory, and Gold. They brought tyranny and slaughter to the New World, along with Catholicism and the colorism that sets those with lighter skin, suggesting Spanish ancestral background, above those with darker skin, reflecting indigenous heritage.

It is here that I left the march and Patti, taking some comfort in the knowledge that she will continue to undo some small pieces of this tragedy. We live among wreckage and monuments, I thought, and at least some people are working tirelessly to build a better future where our monuments might be to justice and equity.

Epilogue: Traces of Blood and Tears

The road to Puerta del Diablo, a mountain crag that resembles a devil's face, is winding and slow. It is about an hour from downtown San Salvador.

Near the top of the hill, there is a turnout where during the war the death squads, the military, and the police would take the bodies of those whom they had swept off the street and killed. They would toss the bodies onto the rocks below, and by morning the vultures would be picking at the softest parts. Grieving families would come here to look for loved ones who had disappeared.

Joan Didion wrote about this spot in her 1983 book *Salvador.* "Nothing fresh today, I hear," an embassy officer says when Didion mentions she had visited Puerta del Diablo the day before. "Were there any on top?" someone else asked. "There were supposed to be three on top yesterday." Its function, in other words, was well-known.

I tried to travel to this spot in 2023 with my fellow journalist Tom Johnson and driver Roger. (Che and his wife had immigrated back to his wife's native Holland.) At first, we drove right past it. Up the hill, we asked for directions from a woman decked in motorcycle gear and parked by the side of the road.

There was a reason, we learned, that we had driven right past it: On the turnout where the dumping used to take place, a new hotel, restaurant, and bodegas were being built—big, fancy, and with spectacular views of the valleys below. It seemed that there would be no plaque here, no sign of the grim past.

As we had turned and twisted up the road, I kept imagining what it would have been like if you were still alive and being taken to your death. You'd wonder how many more turns were ahead until the stopping place was reached, how many more breaths you might take. Fear would probably drive your bowels to move. If it was in the spring, maybe just before Holy Week, you would hear the overwhelming, high-pitched screech of the mating *chicharras*, a type of cicada whose buzz makes it the loudest insect in the world. The buzz would cover the screams of the nightly victims.

The dumping ground's repurposing for commerce seems of a piece with the country's wider approach to the past. Although the Truth Commission represented a courageous effort at reckoning with the war, on a day-to-day basis, its ravages seemed to be getting locked in a dark past.

Or perhaps this is just what it looks like as time passes, and things change. When I arrived at the Salvador airport in 1981 with a bulletproof vest under my cheap sports coat, the place was crowded, hot, and smelly, and all the cab drivers seemed ominous. Today there are new terminals, new gates, new facilities, and the taxi drivers wait in a pleasant courtyard filled with trees and seem very polite.

At the majestic Metropolitan Cathedral of San Salvador, in the main square downtown, the Sunday mass is full of worshippers. A large portrait of Archbishop Romero, who was canonized in 2018, surrounded by children graces the entry to the chancel. The Metropolitan Cathedral was the scene of two mass shootings by soldiers and security forces, one in May 1979 when soldiers opened fire on protesters inside the church, and another when more than 40 people were killed by security forces in 1980 during Romero's funeral. As you walk down the steps of the Church to the central plaza, you can see where the soldiers who carried out the shooting had perched on the roof of the National Palace.

But what seizes your attention as you walk through the plaza is a monster building, looking like a beast ready to pounce on the square and gobble it in one bite, and the cathedral right across the plaza about to be snapped up in a second bite. It is the new national library being built with $54 million in nonreimbursable loans from the People's Republic of China, which is not discreet in promoting its good deed. On fences in front of the building, the benefactors are proclaimed and appreciated.

The U.S. justified its involvement in the Salvadoran Civil War as part of a global fight against communism. Today, in addition to building a new modern library on San Salvador's most notable community space, China—the largest and most powerful communist country in the world—is also financing a new water system at Lake Ilopango, a tourist dock at La Libertad, and a national stadium.

The funding arrived in part because of Nayib Bukele, who took office as president of El Salvador in 2019. A former member of the FMLN, Bukele was elected in 2019 on a platform that involved a monumental repudiation of the past, including turning his back on the established political parties of the left and the right, instituting a massive crackdown on suspected gang members, and taking radical economic measures. He declared El Salvador a Bitcoin economy and urged Bitcoin entrepreneurs to come to El Salvador. He announced he was going to run for reelection, despite the fact that the constitution allows only one term. He overhauled the court system to give more power to the president and fired the attorney general. And as murders among and by gang members rose, Bukele undertook a campaign of mass arrests, sending military units into communities like Soyapango, which was cordoned off from the rest of the city, to round up anybody they suspected of being a gang member. Under what Bukele has declared a "state of exception," more than 60,000 people, mostly men, have been imprisoned, largely without due process, in a clear violation of international human rights law.

Many Salvadorans approve of this crackdown, including our new driver and translator, Roger Hernandez, who was a wonderful member of our team. On the days he drove for us, he would leave his home in Santa Ana and drive for two hours until he hit San Salvador traffic. Then he could be stuck for up to an hour. ("We had guns; now we have traffic," he joked once.) But even after sitting in traffic for three hours, he would greet us cheerfully, interested and always obliging our research requests.

Roger gave us an interesting bio. On one day, he told us he had been in the Salvadoran military and rose to the rank of colonel. On another day, he said he had been a Salvadoran Marine and was aware of an incident I had covered in 1981 involving Nicaraguan sailors fleeing their homeland to El Salvador. On a third occasion, he said he had studied at the Monterey Language Institute, a U.S. military training area for specialized forces that needed training in languages like Farsi, or Arabic, or Russian. He said he studied military logistics. The different stories all meant he had been on one side in the civil war and probably had played a key role. But we did not go into details. We were following a tradition of not getting too close to the bad memories of the '80s and '90s.

Our deal with Roger was $100 per day, gas, and lunch. When it came to lunch, we bickered like college boys in a sports bar. Nobody would say what they wanted to eat. So one day, Roger pulled into the nearest hole-in-the-wall and ordered deep-fried tilapia. I did the same, adding a chicken gumbo dish, while Tom, a vegetarian, ordered fried rice, vegetables, and sopapilla. Total cost, with Cokes, was $10.

I watched as Roger ate the tilapia. Not a piece of flesh remained when he finished, and the bones were attached in perfect order off the head of the fish. On my plate: a mess of flesh on the tilapia, and a pile of chicken and fish bones almost as large as my total serving.

On a cool evening on that same trip, Tom Johnson and I went to meet with Leslie Schuld. Schuld has spent more than 30 years in El Salvador. She came to repair the damage that was caused by the civil war. In the years since, she has helped rebuild communities devastated by tropical floods. She has taken on multinational mining companies eager to exploit resources in remote communities that have little political power. And she has organized multinational election monitors while running a language school for the young and old from around the world.

She has also faced death threats, including one from a businessman whose hotel is just a block from her house. She has stood up to government officials and rallied the poorest of the poor. These days, every night from 7 until 10 p.m., or sometimes as late as midnight, she waits outside a detention center, called El Penalito, or "Little Prison," not far from where she lives. She took us to her post, across a wide boulevard from the holding facility.

Late every afternoon, the government releases a list of who will be released at El Penalito. Along the sidewalk, Schuld pointed out the family members who had been told their men were being released from what has become the largest lockup in Central American history. Schuld had seen a name on the daily list that was similar to one of 22 young men arrested without cause during the gang crackdown on the small eastern El Salvador island of Espíritu Santo. "They were not gang members," she explained. "There are no gang members on that island," which is filled with coconut groves in the bay of Jiquilisco. So far, Centro de Intercambio y Solidaridad and its supporters have won the release of four islanders, and two have the paperwork for release. "This is what solidarity is," she said. She hoped one would be free that night and wanted to make sure there would be somebody there to greet him, find him clothes, and get him to shelter. But he was not among the 10 released.

At the main prison, which Bukele has named the Terrorism Confinement Center, the arrested are crammed up to 600 to a cell. Their meals are sparse and must be paid for by families and friends on the outside. They are forced to wear baggy white shirts and underwear instead of pants. The system is designed to demoralize the prisoners and chip away at their sense of selfhood.

In the wake of the arrests, the murder rate has dropped and many Salvadorans say the streets are safer. The result is that Bukele, at age 42, is supported by 80 percent of the population, which makes him the most popular leader in Latin America. Yet human rights groups in El Salvador and around the world are critical of the crackdown, alleging serious mistreatment of prisoners. But the most powerful argument is that most of those arrested are never charged, have no court dates, and have no process to win release.

A woman running a makeshift sidewalk waiting room warned people not to take pictures of the prisoners in their baggy white underwear when they are just released. But one young reporter, Zoila, from the women's website *Alharaca* (it translates as "fuss"), discreetly took some shots anyway, and her pictures were soon on the *Alharaca* website. She and one other reporter from *Alharaca* there that night struck me as one possible, more hopeful future of El Salvador, with a free press run by women fighting for equality and dignity. They seemed fearless. Their reporting is meant to keep the issue of the mass arrests alive and to illustrate the demeaning actions of the authorities. The admonition to not take pictures is not about privacy; it is a way of controlling what is being broadcast about the roundups.

Schuld recalled being a first-year student at the University of Dayton, learning first about the killing of the nuns on the highway, and then the assassination of Archbishop Romero. "That really shook me up," she says. Her Puerto Rican roommate convinced her to attend a lecture by Father Roy Bourgeois, a critic of U.S. training at Fort Benning for Salvadoran military officers. Later, these same officers were implicated in both random killings and entire massacres.

Schuld, for her part, worked in ways that sought to atone for those crimes. She became a volunteer in the anti-war movement, and her leadership skills and commitment to the cause led her to one powerful position after another. She eventually became the national program director for CISPES, a national Salvadoran support group.

"I remember talking at one point about what would happen after the war," she said. The Peace Accords were signed in 1994. The anti-war groups in the U.S. went on to cut staff, she said, "because people will give donations when there is a war, but not when there is peace." So she decided to organize a post-war support organization, Centro de Intercambio y Solidaridad (CIS). "It was not easy," she said. They started with a scholarship and university leadership program in San Salvador. "We were not a charity," she asserted. "We are solidarity."

At times, she says, she is disheartened by the state of El Salvador today. "In 1932, they were killing peasants, then they were killing guerrillas, and now they are killing gang members," she said. She said that the declining murder rate in El Salvador is an "illusion," because the government does not count the gang members killed by the police or military. And even though "you don't see gang members on every corner," she said, "that doesn't mean they are not there." Moreover, it's not at all clear when or whether the more than 60,000 incarcerated young people will be released—Bukele has threatened to lock them up "forever"—or what will happen if they are released. It is not just sons who are being locked up, but also fathers and uncles, depriving thousands of families of their breadwinners. Critics of the crackdown also point to evidence from similar mass arrests in Latin America for the growth of even more sinister gangs inside the prisons.

It is with great reluctance that I return to Agua Caliente and the power plant with Roger and Tom. They want to see it. I don't. They are curious about the site; I thought I had visited it for the last time. I finally agree but do so feeling sick about it. It takes forever to get there in the traffic, and Roger gets lost. We stop four different times for directions and are given four different routes. When we finally get to the spot, just up from the power station, I no longer know where Gilberto fell. Tom wants to take a photo of me standing in the street. It is the last thing I want to do. It is time for me to move on.

On this trip, we stayed at the Sheraton in the Colonia San Benito in order to catch the 5:45 a.m. Pullmantur bus to Guatemala to write and relax. It has a gorgeous pool, which is said to be the biggest and best at any hotel in San Salvador. It is hard to imagine that this hotel was once owned by one of the funders of the death squads, who had three American aid workers murdered as they sat on the patio. Today, the patio offers relief from the big city. The buses come and go. The businesspeople check in and check out. They give you a drink ticket on check-in, but Tom can't get the bar to honor it.

Next door is the spectacular Museum of Art of El Salvador, known as the Mardi Museum. There are many pieces of art that are dark and foreboding, filled with scenes depicting grief and loss. But the museum is also filled with exhibits of spectacular joy and beauty. It is seen as a monument to El Salvador's future and the creative powers of its people.

At 5 a.m. on my final morning in San Salvador, I sat in the hotel's bus terminal awaiting the Pullmantur bus to Guatemala City, wanting to find out more about the upcoming presidential election, which pits a reformist against a representative of the ruling elite. As each new passenger entered the waiting room, they would say "Buenos días" to those already waiting, and the entire crowd would answer in unison, "Buenos días." I was touched by this display of collective friendliness and mutual recognition. It was hard to imagine a similar scene playing out in the United States, least of all in a bus station.

I still have not found Gilberto's grave—and what if I did? I would stare at it, take a picture, maybe look to see who else was buried nearby. It would not bring redemption or forgiveness. But even without that, I realized, I'd cast my lot in part with the living—working to recognize them, to value and support their good work. I feel proud of my small part assisting DRI with their aid to La Chacra and Cinquera. And I have met so many kind and generous Salvadorans and Americans working to rebuild this tiny country.

Ray Bonner ends his book *Weakness and Deceit* by noting that the one person in the U.S. government who told the truth about the Salvadoran government and military cover-ups of the death squads, the murder of Americans, and the huge toll of civilians killed in military operations, Salvador Ambassador Robert White, was fired and forced out of the diplomatic service. Bonner's conclusion? "No American official has been held to account for the crimes committed by the American-backed governments in El Salvador, or for the deceit emanating from Washington."

I don't know how to make that change, but I do know that I want to keep trying, to atone not just for Gilberto's death, but for my country's actions. Maybe this book will inspire others to embrace our neighbors, our brothers and sisters, of El Salvador, and to keep working to right the wrongs.

SALVADORAN PRESS CORPS ASSOCIATION

JUNTA PROVISIONAL

Bernard Diederich
EXECUTIVE SECRETARY 1

Donald Critchfield
EXECUTIVE SECRETARY 2

Alejandro Benes
EXECUTIVE DIRECTOR

Robin Lloyd
DIRECTOR LOGISTICS

Chris Dickey
DIRECTOR SPORTS

Mark Seibel
FOREIGN AFFAIRS

Godofredo Guedes

Michael Boetcher

Kathy Hersch

John Hoagland

Elizabeth Nissen

John Newhagen

Alon Reininger

David Miller

Eloy Aguilar

Joe Frazier

Gary Pedersen

Al Maldonado

Bill Landrey

Juan Tamayo

Guy Gugliotta

Ike Seamans

Carlos Rosas

Howard J. Dorf

David K. Shanahan

Al Kamen

Tom Buckley

John McClintock

Alex Brody

Eduardo Vasquez Becker

Zoe Trujillo

Jackie Griffin

Bernard Nudelman

Roberto Moreno

Carl Sorensen

Mark Stoddard

Manuel Alvarez

Alma Guillermo Prieto

Harvey Reinsma

Nicholas Asheshov

Patrick Hamilton

Bert Pacas

Charles Gomez

Steve Born

Carl Hersch

Bernard Nudelman
July 1, 2015 ·

We served.

Never too much for a barefoot Salvadoran boy. Photo by Brad Kazmerzak.

Acknowledgements

My wife, Denise, and our three beautiful children: Kendra (the interpreter), George IV (the adventurer) and Lincoln (the webmaster). Ken Leake, for having the guts to send me to El Salvador. Leslie Schuld, for all her help. Luis Alfredo "Che" Alvarado and Roger Hernandez, for driving me safely; Noel Greenwood, for early edits; Megan Pugh, for brilliant work on the manuscript; Tom Johnson and Brad Kazmerzak, for photos and being true *compañeros*; Steve Patten and Larry Bullard, and Tony Foresta, for taking me in at the Camino Real; Kelsey Brugger, for writing help; the late Douwe Stuurman, who shared the pleasures of writing and the late Noel Greenwood for his first important edit of this book; John Weiss, for supporting my work; Tessa Reeg, for gifted proofreading, and Dianne Travis-Teague, for her last look; Steve Metzger, Larry Jackson, and David Hurst, for helping me get to press; Connie Rutherford, for making sure I made it; Natalie Wong, for her cartography; Dan Smith and Thomas Tighe with Direct Relief International, for their trust in my courier work; Diane Joy Schmidt, for sharing her important photos.

And the people of El Salvador who guided me, counseled me, and demonstrated the power of forgiveness.

Recommended Reading

Arnson, Cynthia, *El Salvador: A Revolution Confronts the United States*, Institute for Policy Studies

Barnert, Elizabeth, *Reunion: Finding the Disappeared Children of El Salvador*, University of California Press

Böll, Heinrich, *A Los Que Ya No Están...*, Fundación Heinrich Böll

Bosch, Brian, *The Salvadoran Officer Corps and the Final Offensive of 1981*, McFarland & Co.

Carrigan, Ana, *Salvador Witness: The Life and Calling of Jean Donovan*, Simon & Schuster

Ching, Erik, *Stories of Civil War in El Salvador*, University of North Carolina Press

Clements, Dr. Charles, *Witness to War*, Bantam Books

Danner, Mark, *The Massacre at El Mozote*, Vintage Books

Didion, Joan, *Salvador*, Washington Square Press

Diskin, Martin and Kenneth Sharpe, *The Impact of U.S. Policy in El Salvador, 1979–85*, Institute of International Studies, University of California

D'Haeseleer, Brian, *The Salvadoran Crucible: The Failure of U.S. Counterinsurgency in El Salvador 1979–92*, University Press of Kansas

D'Aubuisson, Juan Jose Martinez, *A Year Inside MS-13: See, Hear, and Shut Up*, OR Books

Eisenbrandt, Matt, *Assassination of a Saint*, University of California Press

Farina, Laura Pedraza and Spring Miller and James Cavallaro, *No Place to Hide: Gang, State, and Clandestine Violence in El Salvador*, Harvard University Press

Forche, Carolyn, *What You Have Heard Is True*, Bantam Books

Forche, Carolyn, *The Country Between Us*, Harper Perennial

Forche, Carolyn and Harry Mattison, Susan Meiselas, Fae Rubenstein, *El Salvador: Work of Thirty Photographers*, Writers and Readers Publishing Cooperative

François, David, *El Salvador: Volume 1: Crisis, Coup and Uprising 1970–1983*, Helion & Co.

Frazier, Joseph, *El Salvador Could Be Like That*, Karina Library Press

Gasteazoro, Ana Margarita, *Tell Mother I'm in Paradise: Memoirs of a Political Prisoner in El Salvador*, University of Alabama Press

Gettleman, Marvin, and Patrick Lacefield, and Louis Menashe, and David Mermelstein, and Ronald Radosh, *El Salvador: Central America in the New Cold War*, Grove Press

Gould, Jeffrey and Aldo Lauria-Santiago, *To Rise in Darkness: Revolution, Repression, and Memory in El Salvador 1920–1932*, Duke University Press

Greentree, Todd, *Crossroads of Intervention: Insurgency and Counterinsurgency Lessons from Central America*, Naval Institute Press

Ladutke, Lawrence, *Freedom of Expression in El Salvador: The Struggle for Human Rights and Democracy*, McFarland & Co.

Logan, Samuel, *This Is for the Mara Salvatrucha: Inside the MS-13, America's Most Violent Gang*, Hyperion

Lovato, Roberto, *Unforgetting: A Memoir of Family, Migration, Gangs, and Revolution in the Americas*, HarperCollins

Markey, Eileen, *A Radical Faith: The Assassination of Sister Maura*, Nation Books

MacDonald, Mandy and Mike Gatehouse, *In the Mountains of Morazán: Portrait of a Returned Refugee Community in El Salvador*, Latin American Bureau

McConahay, Mary Jo, *Ricochet: Two Women War Reporters and a Friendship Under Fire*, SheBooks

Meiselas, Susan, *On the Frontline*, Aperture

Mendoza, Humberto, *El Salvador, El Pueblo, Su Lucha*, Colectivo de Comunicación**

Montgomery, Tommie Sue, *Revolution in El Salvador: From Civil Strife to Civil Peace*, Westview Press

Moodie, Ellen, *El Salvador in the Aftermath of Peace*, University of Pennsylvania Press

Mosure, Patricia and Stephen Patten, *Foreign Correspondent: A Journalist's True Story*, Lee & Grant International

Penate, Oscar Martinez and Maria Elena Sanchez, *El Salvador Diccionario*, Editorial Nuevo Enfoque**

Perez, Orlando, *Historical Dictionary of El Salvador*, Rowman and Littlefield

Randall, Margaret, *Women Brave in the Face of Danger*, Crossing Press

Romero, Edgar, et. al, *El Salvador 10 Años Después: Una Historia Rebelada 1992–2002*, Association Equipo Maíz**

Romero, Edgar, et. al, *Imágenes Para No Olvidar: El Salvador 1900–1999*, Association Equipo Maíz**

Sprenkels, Ralph, *After Insurgency: Revolution and Electoral Politics in El Salvador*, University of Notre Dame Press

Stanley, William, *The Protection Racket State*, Temple University Press

Ucles, Mario, *El Salvador in the Eighties: Counterinsurgency and Revolution*, Temple University Press

Venter, Al, *El Salvador: Dance of the Death Squads, 1980–92*, Pen & Sword Military

Viterna, Jocelyn, *Women in War: The Micro-Processes of Mobilization in El Salvador*, Oxford University Press

Wade, Christine, *Captured Peace: Elites and Peacebuilding in El Salvador*, Ohio University Press

Wheeler, William, *State of War: MS-13 and El Salvador's World of Violence*, Columbia Global Reports

Whitfield, Teresa, *Paying the Price: Ignacio Ellacuría and the Murdered Jesuits of El Salvador*, Temple University Press

Wood, Elisabeth Jean, *Insurgent Collective Action and Civil War in El Salvador*, Cambridge University Press

Wright, Scott, *Promised Land: Death and Life in El Salvador*, Orbis Books

Zagano, Phyllis, *Ita Ford: Missionary Martyr*, Paulist Press

Zugibe, Frederick and David Carroll, *Dissecting Death: Secrets of a Medical Examiner*, Broadway Books

**Spanish

George Thurlow Personal Bibliography on Latin America

AlterNet: Sept. 11, 2000: "The Militarization of El Salvador"

Feedback: The California Journalism Review: Summer 1981: "A Shooting in El Salvador"

Chico News & Review: Mar. 25, 1982: "They Shoot (And Kill) Journalists Don't They"

Chico News & Review: Jan. 21, 1982: "Wealth and Revolution Boiling in Mexico"; "El Salvador Election Will Kill Candidates"

Chico News & Review: Sept. 16, 1982: "A New Society in a Troubled Region"

Chico News & Review: Sept. 30, 1982: "Nicaragua: The Americans"

Chico News & Review: Apr. 11, 1985: "Is Mexico Safe for American Tourists?"

Chico News & Review: June 9, 1983: "Regional War Spills into Mexico"

Fresno Bee: May 17, 1981: "Terror Reign: 22,000 Are Slaughtered in Salvador Political Turmoil"

San Francisco Bay Guardian: Aug. 30, 2000: "Militarizing El Salvador"

Sacramento Bee: Oct. 3, 1982: "Sabotage, Armed Raids in Nicaragua Appear Up in Wake of Covert U.S. Aid"

Sacramento Bee: Nov. 13, 1982: "Nicaragua Struggles After the Revolution"

Sacramento Bee: May 17, 1981: "Suspicion, Death Stalk Salvadorans"

Sacramento Bee: Jan. 24, 1982: "Davis Woman's Brother Missing in El Salvador"

Sacramento Bee: Jan. 24, 1982: "Exiles Deplore Terrorism in El Salvador"

San Francisco Chronicle and *Examiner*: May 24, 1981: "Eyewitness Story of Ambush in El Salvador"

San Diego CityBeat: July 5, 2006: "On the Path to Democracy: A Teetering Mexico Lurches Toward a Genuine Representative Government"

Santa Barbara Independent: June 26, 2002: "Salvadoran Coffee: The Bitter Grind of a Worldwide Glut"
Santa Barbara Independent: June 9, 2005: "El Salvador: No Easy Solution"
Santa Barbara Independent: Dec. 21, 2000: "Taking Christmas to El Salvador: The Journey of one Relief Box from Santa Barbara to La Chacra"
Santa Barbara Independent: Aug. 12, 2004: "Deadline Line in the Sand: The Ever Rising Cost in Dollars and Lives of American Border Policies"

Santa Barbara News & Review: Nov. 11, 1982: "The Squeeze on Nicaragua"
Santa Barbara News & Review: Oct. 7, 1982: "Report from Nicaragua"
Santa Barbara News & Review: May 14, 1981: "Just an El Salvador Mistake"
Santa Barbara News & Review: Jan. 28, 1982: "From the Barrel of a Gun"
Santa Barbara News & Review: Nov. 4, 1982: "Nicaragua's Other Americans"
Santa Barbara News & Review: Oct. 21, 1982: "Nicaragua Faces the Contras"

The Press: August 1981: "The Story of One Who Lived."

Time: Sept. 5, 1994: "Mexico: The People's Choice (Honest)"

New Haven Advocate: June 3, 1981: "A Mistake in El Salvador"

New West: July 1981: "El Salvador Is No Place to Be Young"

Vacaville Reporter: May 13, 1981: "Stay and I Die, Get Up and Die.
    I Run"
Vacaville Reporter: May 17, 1981: "Ravages of War, and Constant
    Fear of Death Among Poor"

Woodland *Daily Democrat*: May 11, 1981: "Ambush Survivor's
    Report from El Salvador"
Woodland *Daily Democrat*: May 13, 1981: "Salvador Refuge from
    the Storm of War"
Woodland *Daily Democrat*: May 14, 1981: "Bitterness Marks El
    Salvador Ag Reform"
Woodland *Daily Democrat*: May 15, 1981: "El Salvador: A
    Journalist's Nightmare"
Woodland *Daily Democrat*: May 16, 1981: "You Have Seen
    Violence and Repression"

About the Author

George Thurlow has worked as a reporter, editor, university journalism lecturer, publisher and writer since 1974. His coverage of Latin America has appeared in numerous newspapers and magazines across the U.S. He has served as the president of the California Society of Newspaper Editors and the chair of the California Newspaper Publishers Foundation. He currently serves on the board of directors of the UC Press Foundation and is treasurer of the national Alternative Newsweekly Foundation. His reporting has appeared in the *Los Angeles Times, Sacramento Bee, San Francisco Examiner, Time* magazine, the Associated Press, the *Columbia Journalism Review* and numerous other magazines and newspapers.

Printed in the USA
CPSIA information can be obtained
at www.ICGtesting.com
CBHW032117011124
16698CB00001B/5